BIKE! Motorcycles and the People Who Ride Them

BIKE! Motorcycles

and the People Who Ride Them

THIERRY SAGNIER

HARPER & ROW, PUBLISHERS
NEW YORK, EVANSTON, SAN FRANCISCO, LONDON

FIRST EDITION

Designed by C. Linda Dingler

Library of Congress Cataloging in Publication Data
Sagnier, Thierry.
    Bike! Motorcycles and the people who ride them.
    1. Motorcycling—United States—History.
    2. Motorcycles—History. I. Title.
GV1059.5.S23   796.7′5   72-9151
ISBN 0-06-013736-3
ISBN 0-06-013743-6 (pbk.)

To Barbara and Elizabeth,
for our future.

Contents

Illustrations

Page

Acknowledgments

In my research and writing of this book, I have been helped by many people, too many to thank individually. My thanks to all of them, particularly to Michael F. Parks for friendship and aid when needed, to Robert Wool for giving me a start, and to my editors Peter Burling and Harold Grove for permitting me to finish.

BIKE! Motorcycles and the People Who Ride Them

1

Images, Myths, and Realities

A long, long time ago, back in 1953, Columbia Pictures released a movie portraying a brooding young man raising hell on a motorcycle. The movie, entitled *The Wild One*, was loosely based on events that came to pass in Hollister, California, in 1947 and starred a 650 c.c. Triumph, a black-leather jacket, and Marlon Brando in that order. It featured a lot of sighing, a few immortally grunted lines—"My old man hit harder than that"—and was the first serious attempt to portray the nascent motorcycle culture as a threat to all that was good, decent, and organized.

The plot was rather insipid. Marlon Brando leads a bunch of motor-cyclists into a small town. They raise hell. They fight another bunch of motorcyclists who by their very appearance are even worse than Brando's bunch. Then Brando falls in love with the sheriff's daughter, gets stomped by the irate townsfolk, and in the end really proves to be not such a bad guy, particularly for a biker.

Bosley Crowther, of the New York *Times*, wrote an inimitable review full of sound, fury, and applicable phrases like "glandular psycho," "dope

In July of 1947, between 2,000 and 4,000 motorcyclists roared into the small California town of Hollister, California, to attend the American Motorcycle Association sponsored, annual "gypsy tour." The ensuing three days made headlines, and, several years later, were the basis for a film that made Marlon Brando famous as the star of *The Wild One*.

fiend," and "fantastically mad" and capsuled the entire presentation by writing:

The subject of its [the movie's] examination is a swarm of youthful motorcyclists who ride through the country in wolf-pack fashion and terrorize the people of one small town. Given to jive or be-bop lingo and the grotesque costumes and attitudes of the "crazy" cognoscenti, these "wild ones" resent discipline and show an aggressive contempt for decency and the police. Reckless and vandalistic, they live for sensations, nothing more—save perhaps the supreme sensation of defying the normal world.

Crowther's review totally missed the entire point of the movie, overlooking or ignoring the overdone implications of alienation, dichotomy, and paradoxes in a manner surprising for a professional cinema critic.

But no matter. The seed was sown. *The Wild One* made history. What

The motorcyclists, gathering here for a three-day program of social activities, began "taking over the town" the evening of July 3.

Mr. Crowther did not realize, and what apparently no one realized, was that the picture would influence a large number of people.

Like the youths who, during the Depression, idolized Al Capone, Ma Barker, Babyface Nelson and who would undoubtedly have elected John Dillinger to the governorship of almost any state, the youths of the 1950s desperately sought to escape the apathy of their time, and were ready and ripe to follow Brando's lead, which simultaneously typecast for more than a decade and a half the motorcycle image.

There weren't too many Marlon Brandos and even fewer "crazy cognoscenti" at the time of the filming. A small number of motorcycle packs were roaming around the West Coast, not really destroying anything but scaring the bejesus out of the local citizenry and generally riling the authorities. But there was no notoriety, no *Saturday Evening Post* cover stories and cheap nickel-and-dime movies eulogizing wheeled freedom and violence.

The great majority riding at that time were simply folks, nonviolent ones whose most heinous crimes were exceeding the speed limit and shattering the night's silence. The existing gangs were mostly composed of Okie and Arkie types who'd discovered that motorcycles were far cheaper and more thrilling than 1947 chopped-and-blown Mercury sedans. They wore Air Force Surplus leather flight jackets because it gets awfully cold doing sixty or seventy miles an hour in winter, and the pavement hurts when you miss the curve on a back country road. Leather cushioned the fall and was easier to replace than skin. They wore blue jeans because they were cheap and didn't tear easily, heavy boots that wouldn't need resoling after a couple of miles of high-speed foot dragging. They sported little leather caps to keep the hair out of their eyes and preserve the carefully groomed Brylcreme look.

The leather jacket and Harley became the symbol of the hood, the greaser, the slightly mad, smirking one who destroyed and raped like a wheeled Atilla the Hun.

In the summer of 1969, Columbia Pictures again released a movie starring a motorcycle and a brooding young man. Peter Fonda and his sidekick on outrageous 1,200 c.c. Harley-Davidson choppers make their bundle selling a white powder that could be heroin or cocaine, then take off cross-country for the Mardi Gras in New Orleans, staring at sunsets and sighing a lot. Toward the end, they're gunned down by two good old Southern boys who, it's understood, travel in a pick-up truck with shotguns slung

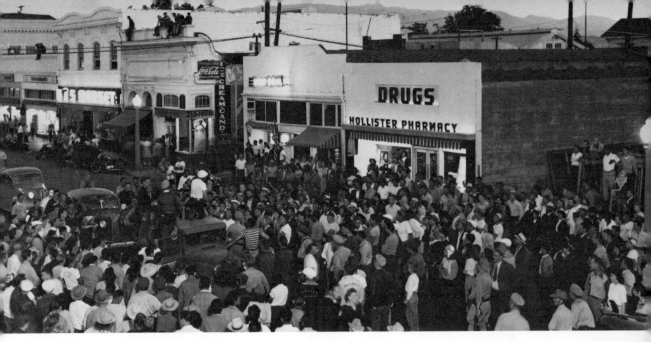

Hundreds of individuals who invaded the town for the motorcycle show, halted their riotous "play" to dance.

Shortly after dusk, the force of forty highway patrol officers, commanded by Captain L. T. Torres of San Benito County, forced a lull in the terrorism.

The attitude of the motorcyclists was expressed by one youth today in the words: "Well, the American Legion goes into a town and raises hell. It's a convention. We're just having a convention . . ."

The "gypsy tour" was sponsored by the Salinas Ramblers Motorcycle Club and the Hollister Veteran's Memorial Park Association.

Armed with tear guns, the officers herded the cyclists into a block on San Benito street.

across the rear window, searching for errant long-hairs and wasting them without looking back.

What the acting and plot line lacked was made up by the photography and timeliness of the presentation. In a time of largely nonviolent rebellion, the movie couldn't help but make it. It was, after all, an almost-first attempt by the youth of the country to hit the masses with visual art and leave a visible and talented track across the celluloid garbage appearing in most neighborhood theaters. It was also one of the first movies about youth's "struggle" to coexist peacefully with the elements it defied.

Fonda struck a softer note than Brando, that of a mellower, largely peaceful, and noninvolved personality. Like Brando, he was misunderstood, his motives misinterpreted. But Brando instigated violence in spite of himself. Fonda was its victim—the acid-headed, freaked- and dropped-out child of *The Wild One.*

Few people realized the "hip" meaning of the movie's title—an "easy rider" is a man who lives off the profits his woman makes by prostituting herself—and the Easy Rider syndromes comfortably outlined the "in" things of the mid and late sixties: alienation, loss, search, drugs, speed, sex, noninvolvement, the whole underlined by a constant trace of violence.

The legend grew. Captain Americas and Billys crisscrossed the land in Stars and Stripes helmets atop red, white, and blue motorcycles. Few ever met Fonda's untimely end, and some reported that things just weren't like that at all. Sure, some rednecks gave long-hairs a rough time now and then, but down in Macon, Georgia, you could always sleep in the jail and the sheriff's wife would probably fix you breakfast. But the image was set and remained, even if it didn't conform to the realities of the times. It fit the frame of mind of a certain generation, and motorcycles became for many the instruments of freedom, a wild freedom, for sure, a slightly reckless, slightly insane one, but a freedom nevertheless. The fifteen years separating *The Wild One* from *Easy Rider* saw the motorcycle become almost but not quite socially acceptable, largely replacing the channeled and fuel-injected Model T with the candy-apple paint job. And in that decade and a half, it became a new way to get there and back, a Holy Grail, a way of life second to none, an all-consuming passion.

The motorcycle is by definition anti-American. It's a direct insult to Naugahyde upholstery and padded dashboards, push-button windows and power brakes. It's a reaction against waste, frills, planned obsolescence, and the buy-a-new-one-a-year marketing techniques practiced by virtually all auto makers. It defies the increasing "safety first" trend, for it is conceived with elemental simplicity in mind: two wheels, an engine, a seat, and a frame to hold the whole together, horsepower to get the wheels moving, and multispeed gearboxes to demultiply and stretch that power beyond the realm of most imaginations and temerity. Comfort sacrificed for mobility. Falsely streamlined looks and added weight by-passed for speed and handling.

The bike essentially represents a return to the rudiments of traveling. Go light, go fast, unencumbered by two tons of metal dragging beneath and around you. Magic wheels stuck to your tail. Back to the wind-in-the-face days, back to the sheer, gutsy, spine-tingling speed, and, more important, the total awareness of that speed.

And back, too, to the lost skills that once were needed to get from here to there. A big bike, as opposed to a big car, needs a certain amount of

Some fifty persons were jailed during the ruckus. "If we'd jailed everyone who deserved it, we'd have herded them in by the hundreds," police said.

This biker qualifies as one of the earliest motorcycle rowdies. Though he is unidentified, his picture was featured in *Life* magazine no less than twice, and his drunken, if not fearsome, countenance was enough to instill in thousands of people a fear of motorcycles. He is the direct predecessor of Marlon Brando in *The Wild One.*

strength and knowledge to be handled competently. Vibrations, jars, and bumps are not lost somewhere between the shock absorbers and the spring-mounted, foam-padded reclining buckets. Only a small percentage are sponged by the seat. The rest are received by the rider's knees, arms, and backbone. Though hydraulic disc brakes and clutches are presently available on many modern models, it's still the hand operating the front brake, the body and arms turning the machine. No air-conditioned, water-proofed luxury; no cigarette lighter, either, or one-arm-on-the-window driving with half a mind on the road; the motorcycle, like gliding, skydiving, or bob-sledding is a total-awareness method of moving. It will not brook being ignored or taken for granted like an automobile, since a momentary lack of attention is enough to wipe out the rider permanently. Both hands and both feet are in constant synchronization, constant wakefulness, which might explain why few bikers are prone to highway hypnosis and even fewer fall asleep while riding their machines.

The motorcycle, in the United States as opposed to Europe and Asia, does not fully owe its creation to economic inability to own a saner motor vehicle. In the late fifties and early sixties, they remained cheaper than most sports cars but far more expensive than most automobiles glutting secondhand car lots. They were faster than sedans and had a very definite thing about them, a subtle evil and raunchiness which wasn't lost on the ex-hot rodders who custom-tailored their cars to look mean. The motor-cycle was in fact the direct outgrowth of the hot rod, a post-World War II phenomenon, which, according to different sources, originated in (a) the West Coast, (b) the Dust Bowl, and (c) the South.

The rod was basically an ancient and dilapidated automobile that had been refurbished and made to run again, hopefully, though not always, better, through a series of metallic surgical operations that encompassed body and engine work. In the West, which has always anticipated the rest of the United States' automotive whimsy, the hot rod was no more than the poor man's Cadillac. Take a 1947 Chevrolet, drop a larger engine into it, bore it, stroke it, increase the cam lift, and do funny things with the exhaust. Repaint and upholster it, preferably in a loud and tasteless fashion. Individuality, mobility, and limited expenses were all satisfied. And the rods' performances were fairly mind-blowing. Their speeds were ferocious when compared to the mass-manufactured family cars available, so ferocious, in fact, that a special form of all-American racing was developed simply for them—the quarter-mile-timed acceleration test, the drags, which emphasized brute power above all things, getting down there before anyone else and sacrificing a perfectly good pair of Goodyears in the bargain.

In the Dust Bowl, the rod was an even more economic creation. If you could buy two junkers, hack them up and reglue them into one, you were far better off than the guy next door who had to walk. As a result, the early hot rods of the Dust Bowl were incredible mechanisms held together with string, bailing wire, Calvinistic prayers, and the knowledge accumulated by generations of scrounging.

The Southern rods were perhaps the most interesting if not the most legendary. The Tennessee, Georgia, Virginia, and West Virginia hill country had, since long before Prohibition, been the not-so-secret site of countless illegal liquor stills, which manufactured a few thousand gallons of eye-watering moonshine every year. Once made, the moonshine had to be carried, and daring young drivers ran hare-and-hound races against Internal Revenue Service agents. The agents were usually driving new, high-powered government-issue automobiles. The runners drove decrepit five- and ten-year-old sedans with only one seat, the rest having been removed to allow more liquor space. The runners were caught, arrested, and jailed, losing dignity, employment, and moonshine in one fell swoop. The second time around, the decrepit automobiles outran the revenuers. Intestinal fortitude and countless hours spent tuning, polishing, and milling a worn-out engine made many a mountain boy's Saturday-night liquor run successful, and a few boys even became famous, running their rods in local races, skidding around dirt tracks, and colliding happily in what a few years later became multimillion-dollar spectator sports, the Demolition Derbys and stock-car races.

The hot rod started losing some of its appeal when the pros like Ed Roth began building and marketing highly customized vehicles for a moneyed few willing to pay the tab. The original hot rodders hung on for a time until Detroit struck the death blow by manufacturing factory rods like the Mustang and later its hordes of imitators, powerful beasts with highly tuned V-8 engines, which often could outdrag all but the most persistent home-built competition.

The rodders split. One faction stayed true to automobiles, concentrating their efforts on engine work and eventually turning to Fiberglas or light-alloy bodies for their creations.

The other faction rediscovered motorcycles.

For the motorcycle was not new to the United States and had, much earlier in the century, enjoyed a fair-sized popularity. As early as 1901, the Hendee Manufacturing Company, based in Springfield, Massachusetts, was putting out a single-cylinder contraption called the Indian motorcycle, and, in 1903, the Harley-Davidson Company of Milwaukee, operating from a clapboard shack, had created its first bike.

There are stories told by the very old men who still cherish memories of 1910 Harleys and Excelsiors, tales of cross-country runs that saw bikers outrace hostile American Indians and bands of roving Mexican outlaws intent on bloodletting, stories even then of smuggling pounds of marijuana in rear tires and gas tanks across the Rio Grande, not so much for the money as for the thrill of it all and the opportunity to recount the amplified adventures to the people back home.

A number of smaller companies opened, produced a few dozen vehicles, then closed with little fanfare. A few British bikes were ridden by rich eccentrics who'd traveled overseas and seen what the Limeys were doing.

An early father and son team. The year is 1937 and racer Smoky Dawson is pacing his four-year-old son during an exhibition held prior to sand races in Wallasey, England. The younger Dawson's machine runs off a ½ horsepower engine.

The early years of the war saw a motorcycle manufacturing boom both here and in Europe. Thousands were manufactured by both the Axis and Allied powers. The machines were painted the customary khaki green or brown, coated in vaseline and shipped, girder front end and rigid frame, to fighting units in Europe and Africa. Legend has it that a few caches of these vintage bikes still exist, but the legends for the most part err or are simply disseminated by con men in search of the fast buck.

Flat-track racing on wooden boards or sandy half miles had become a popular and well-attended sport.

But motorcycling in the United States was to suffer an almost fatal setback when, in 1920, a great number of assembly-line automobiles flooded the market.

The cars were far more comfortable than the two-wheeled vehicles they supplanted, far safer and more reliable, and, most important, infinitely more respectable if less sporting.

The cars killed the bikes. Only Harley-Davidson and Indian remained, and motorcycling was taken from a serious means of transportation to a rather foolish hobby and dangerous sport.

And fifty years later, five million motorcycles sputtered, coughed, and wheezed their way across, up, and down the continental United States. The actual number of bikes now in the States is probably far greater than the five million quoted by the American Motorcycle Association. A sizeable proportion of the machines sold are never ridden on the road and, therefore, in many areas need not be registered with state or local authorities.

By the late 1950s and early 1960s, only a few makes were available to the public. Indian folded after an illustrious but losing battle, and Harleys reigned supreme in the States, though their large engines, many lights, automobile tires, and prohibitive prices made them too expensive for many casual riders.

Policemen rode them and one might occasionally spot a three-wheeled delivery vehicle or a red-and-cream-colored motor scooter, which looked suspiciously like a bunch of cardboard boxes painted metallic red.

American Motorcycle Association members rode them, too, but at the time everyone knew that Harley and the AMA had their hands in each other's pockets, and more than one AMA member sported the despised leathers. They also wore the Harley winged cap, which immediately made them suspect.

Harleys, all in all, were too big and too much for the populace to consider them a normal means of transportation.

The European companies were by and large unrepresented, though Nortons, Triumphs, BSAs, and Italian-made Moto-Guzzis were making technological advances overseas. Again, prices in the United States were prohibitive. The $1,000 necessary to purchase a big Limey twin was a bit too extravagant for a hobby.

Then came Honda with *blitzkrieg* advertising aimed both at the consumer's conservatism and pocketbook. The merchandising geniuses of Japan quickly discovered that, in the United States at least, the only way to peddle motorcycles to a brainwashed public was to either destroy the vehicle's bad reputation or re-brainwash potential customers, this time along a different line of thought. This they did.

Billboards and magazine backcovers in stirring colors depicted Clairol-haired maidens in miniskirts astride what by no stretch of the most fertile imagination could accurately be called motorcycles. They were more like

The Japanese invasion hadn't really caught on in the mid-sixties, and most people into touring relied on American machinery: full-dressed Harley-Davidson Electra Glides. Their advantage, of course, is that their size and lasting power enabled you to take the whole family and then some.

motorized bicycles that smoked and made spluttering noises, cost about $300, and needed constant upkeep. It was impossible to envision Marlon Brando straddling one, and a leather jacket or boots were not necessary. A Harley-Davidson cap would have looked ludicrous, since it wasn't a big black, fire-belching monster. It was cute, red, blue, or yellow, largely noise-less, slow, fun, cheap, and socially kinky but acceptable.

The American Honda Motor Company opened up in Gardena, California, a totally unknown company that seemed doomed to failure. The Japanese reputation for cheap imitations that seldom functioned as well as they looked had preceded Honda, and the idea that a corporation, founded by an Oriental who stuffed motors in bicycles, could succeed was preposterous. Americans, after all, had invented advertising, if not the motorcycle. This seemed like another ploy hatched by strange West Coast people.

In 1959 AHMC sold less than $500,000 worth of motorcycles and parts. Seven years later American Honda had multiplied its initial sales 212 times to $106 million. Honda's American success was attributable almost totally to their successful advertising campaign, possibly one of the most successful ever launched in the United States or, for that fact, anywhere else.

Kicked off and run by Grey Advertising, the You Meet The Nicest People on a Honda campaign was double-edged: it strove to dismiss the idea that all riders were hoods and simultaneously implied that you, the buyer, just couldn't be one of those despicable few who tainted the good name of all innocent motorcyclists.

The high-intensity ads, coupled with the low prices quoted for Honda's vehicles, made the cute little things almost irresistable, particularly to the youths who for the first time were coming into money of their own.

The campaign and slogan were far from being a shot in the dark. K. Okumoto, at the time vice-president and general manager of American Honda, said: "We studied the situation very carefully before we moved in in 1959, and we saw that only 50,000 motorcycles a year were being imported into the United States. We saw motorcycles as a cheap form of transportation, especially for students. Right after the war, Japan needed cheap transportation very badly and there was no auto industry to speak of, so people took to bicycles and to the smallest motorcycle made—the engine was only 50 cubic centimeters [author's note: about the size of a drinking glass]. When we moved into California, to start with we brought in our cheapest machines. They cost only $250 compared to $1000 for British machines (author's note: BSA, Triumph, Norton) and $1500 for the American machines on the market at the time (Harley-Davidson)."

The companies already importing motorcycles to the States had preferred to ignore the image attributed to bikers. No attempt had been made to change the public outlook, since the makers did not consider themselves sociologists, and it's rather surprising that Honda was the first to associate respectability with high sales. It was a masterful stroke from which other companies were involuntary beneficiaries, but nevertheless did not recover. Honda then drew another ace and aligned itself with the forces of law, order, and propriety. The Japanese magnate quickly realized that accidents would only harm business, and instructed dealers in the States to implement basic-driving courses with each motorcycle sold.

The courses at the time were the essence of motorcycle safety. Most dealers, too often anxious to move their motorcycles from showroom to street, neglected to instruct the new riders fully on the potential dangers of the shiny new vehicles. The problem was complicated by the major motorcycle manufacturers' insistence on glorified advertising. Yamaha, Kawasaki, Suzuki, and the bigger-bore British machines all strove to portray the motorcycle as a freedom machine. A customer entering his local-dealer's shop entered with this idea in mind, and didn't really care to know the other side of the coin.

Legislators had not yet considered motorcycles as serious modes of transportation and few, if any, laws or regulations existed. A rider was free to ride helmetless, barefoot, and in a bathing suit if he chose to. Many did just that.

The results were to be expected. Thousands straddled various two- or four-stroke motorcycles, reared back on the throttle, popped the clutch, and went careening over hill and dale, through flower beds and rosebush hedges. They generally ended up striking an immovable object, thereby overturning said motorcycle and injuring themselves. The great-car drivers seldom considered them too far removed from kids' bicycles, which, by damn, should stay on the sidewalks where they belonged or face the messy consequences. Riding down the center lane between two cars was an open invitation to disaster. The great majority of injuries, to be sure, were nothing more serious than scraped knees and knuckles, but enough fractured skulls, broken arms, and legs showed up in emergency wards to alarm the medical community and prompt it to issue countless reports on the machine's dangers.

Today's Health magazine in May of 1967 in a story headlined "Your Youngster and the Motorcycle" stated that "what every parent should know is that the death rate for motorcycles is much higher than the comparable rate for automobiles and other motor vehicles. One expert, a civil engineering associate professor, John J. O'Mara of the University of Iowa, estimates that a cyclist has 20 times as much chance of being killed, on a vehicle mile basis. . . . Many times each day in the United States, young people of brilliance and beauty lose one or both of these assets in the impact of their bodies with other vehicles, stationary objects such as poles and fences, dirty roads and ditches."

The professor then went on to illustrate the insanity of it all by describing the outcome of numerous motorcycle accidents all around the land.

The wiser riders had already discovered leathers and helmets, but the newcomers, still hypnotized by the "wind in your ears" school of advertising, rode with little protection until legislation forced them to don hardhats and, in some states, protective clothing and various motorcycle accessories conceived with safety in mind.

Another mistake committed by the industry, one based primarily on greed, was to flood the newly created American market with too much, too soon. Honda, perhaps, tried the hardest to please potential and established customers, yet was certainly the chief perpetrator of the riders' anathema: lack of follow-through.

The American market had proved to be a bonanza, a lodestone, which, according to informed sources, would simply prove to be a trend, like the Hula-Hoop or the Yo-yo. The money was there, for sure, but might not be there tomorrow. Here was the makings of the fast buck, the razzle-dazzle sale. Many companies played "get the sucker," selling barely rideable creations in brilliant colors, never worrying about aftersale service or, for that fact, a dependable shop setup.

Motorcycle mechanics were often ex-gas-pump jockeys who might be able to tell, with luck, a carburetor from a manifold but were totally unable to do even a minor tune-up on a Honda 50 c.c. On the off chance that such a miracle were possible, the great majority of motorcycle dealers never worried about setting up a decent inventory of spare parts.

It wasn't unusual to be stranded for a month, searching for a gasket or a primary gear. An uncounted number of Marushos, Benellis, Gileras, early Honda Sports 50s, and various other little-known machines are probably to this day languishing in dank and dusty garages for lack of an essential 25 cent doodad.

Lest it seem that only the Japanese were responsible for this sad state of affairs, it should be mentioned that the worst culprits of the lot were probably the Italian and British manufacturers.

Italy, long known for incredibly complex and swift racing machinery, hastened to put together a bunch of fairly tacky motorcycles in the hope of making a quick killing on the swelling market. Benelli, for example, exported thousands of 125 c.c. motorcycles, dumping them on the market with little thought of after-sale service. The machines sold, being basically simple two-strokes whose ease of handling could satisfy most riders. But repairs were costly, if possible. Benellis and Gileras eventually came to be represented by major department stores, particularly Sears, Roebuck and Company and Montgomery Ward.

This also turned into a fiasco since few department-store managers were in any way equipped to deal with motorcycles that smoked too much or stuttered or simply stopped. Both stores eventually gave up the idea, but not before realizing a fairly important profit. The riders were left to shift for themselves and Benelli and Gilera virtually vanished from the land.

The British, too, had a hand in the fiasco, exporting powerful 650 c.c. and 750 c.c. machines, which few American motorcycle mechanics could touch.

The problem, incidentally, still exists among the great majority of manufacturers. Honda, in ten years, has presented America with countless new models, sometimes at scant six-month intervals. In 1971 alone, American Honda released more than twenty-two different models, which included three minibikes, two step-thrus, one all-terrain cycle (ATC) two four-cylinder machines, and one mo-ped (motor pedal). A large number of parts, to be sure, are interchangeable, but necessary components like pistons, rings, and cylinders are irreplaceable, made for one model only. If that model suddenly finds itself extinct, well, reason the moguls, *caveat emptor*. "The growth has been so fast," said a Suzuki executive in 1966, "that their just aren't enough mechanics or spares available . . ."

For a few years, the sales of motorcycles in the United States were limited to small- and medium-displacement machines, used mainly for fun and, rationalized some owners, convenience.

The small machines were bought as second vehicles, to be driven only in the fairest of weather. They fulfilled a basic desire to be different, but not too different; to get the impression of speed without, quite often, its reality; to linger in garages when the fun was over. The initial cost of both machine and insurance was small, and, therefore, affordable to many who, without quite knowing why, became the first of the new biker's generation to be hooked on motorcycling. As the machines themselves became more respectable, larger motorcycles were placed on the market and the sports outlook was considered good advertising by the media. Motorcycle racing, which had at one time been highly popular in the States, was again emphasized. Since an incredible number of races were run in Europe and in Japan, it was no great feat to certify that virtually every bike made and exported had, at one time, won a race.

Few advertisers bothered to inform their readers that the machines raced had little in common with the machines sold on the market and that, quite often, the racing machines could not even be bought at any price. They were one-of-a-kind experimental models that cost up to $50,000. Little was said of the men who rode the racing versions, and not many prospective buyers realized that the Yamaguchi Speedster, which according to the ads had done 110 miles per hour through the traps, had been ridden by a ninety-five-pound Japanese drag racer who had spent months trimming tenths and hundredths of seconds from the elapsed time his company so proudly displayed. But it made good copy. College students weaving between cars and buses during rush hours could imitate Italy's Agostini astride a Benelli or Moto-Guzzi. As manufacturers sank greater and greater amounts of money into their advertising budget (Suzuki went from $150,000 in 1964 to $2 million in 1966, while Honda upped its already sizeable budget to $9 million), the Nicest People image was slowly replaced by the Powerful image. Black-leather jackets were still not well looked upon, but who in America could criticize horsepower?

The country had been built upon it, and a good part of the national economy depended on it for its very livelihood. The nation was famed for its wealth of it, its mass manufacturing of it. To badmouth it was almost anti-American, if not at the very least antiprogressive.

The American Achilles' heel was artfully speared with promises of bigger bores, shinier tailpipes, and multiple gears.

By November of 1966, the Japanese imports dominated 85 percent of the American market. The rest was fought over by Harley-Davidson, BSA, Triumph and Berliner imports, which marketed Nortons, BMWs, and Ducatis. The manufacturers of big bikes had admittedly been caught napping. Believing the sales of small machines to be only a fad, they had already lost the market.

There was no such thing as a small BMW, a small Norton, or a small Triumph. All these machines were big, more in line with the bad-guy image than their Japanese counterparts had ever been. And the entire Nicest People campaign had, after all, been centered around the small, harmless Oriental sputterers.

Harley-Davidson tried feebly to make a small motorcycle manufactured in Italy by the Aermacchi people for American consumption. It sold poorly, as did a few British middleweight machines.

But the American way of buying seems whimsical at best, and it is not surprising to see an almost total reversal of trends in a few years. Advertising and research budgets increased, and slicker motorcycle magazines lauded the higher-powered European and American models. Japan's only claim to large displacement at the time came in the way of a Honda 450 c.c., which, though it did cost much less than a full-fledged Harley, was still expensive by most standards. It was also wretched-looking, all angles or obnoxious curves, largely devoid of two things that Americans hold dear—chrome and gaudiness. It seemed to squat on the pavement and was quickly nicknamed The Toad.

Had it been cleaned up and advertised, its sale value would still have been in doubt. If Americans were willing to trust the Japanese for the small sum needed to buy a 50 c.c. or 125 c.c. machine, giving the Japs the sizeable bundle necessary to own a bigger bike was another thing entirely. Everybody knew that Japanese toys were great, but could they come up with the real thing? The time was ripe for the Europeans.

Motorcyclists aboard small displacement machines were getting slightly tired of being outdragged at every red light by tire-squealing Detroit creations. The mood changed, and what the Japanese couldn't offer, the British and Germans did: cubic inches. From 500 c.c. to 750 c.c. of snorting, gas-burning speed, reaching way past the kilo mark and leaving just about everything behind . . . acceleration that could snap your neck back, stand you on the rear wheel scorching the asphalt, sex appeal . . .

For there was nothing sexy about the early Japanese machines. They were cute, true, but not impressive, not impressive at all. You looked collegiate driving around with your girl on the back. Somewhere in the head of most small-bore owners lay the certainty that maybe, if you had a bigger machine, the girl riding behind might be a bit better-looking, or at least hold on tighter during the curves . . .

On a big bore, you looked manly, virile. And you could shut down the neighborhood hood who had a blown 'Vette, leave him standing there looking up your tailpipes.

In fact, the shift from small to big was a natural one. America has always gone to the extreme, whether in its search for money or kicks. The one-color Model A was long gone, and even Detroit had taken the hint and started tailoring its automobile to look fast and sneaky. The average American rider had outgrown the small bike and was ready and eagerly awaiting bigger and better things.

And he didn't have too long to wait.

The Japanese industry dominated by ex-motored bicycle builder Soichiro Honda had never had a chance to develop a large, overpowered machine. Honda's fortune was made, in fact, by providing cheap, afterwar transportation to a nation that drastically needed it.

There was neither time nor money then for speed and frills. The small Japanese machines were Spartan in concept, rarely more than a small engine that permitted the bicycle rider to get to work in relative comfort and not have to fight the hills that cursed his daily trips. Honda and Yamaha had both fought their way to the top of the heap by providing the cheapest form of motorized transportation available.

The Europeans' attempt to launch small machines in America failed utterly. The machines were prehistoric when compared to the Japanese exports: most were two-strokes, which necessitated mixing oil with gasoline, as opposed to the Honda four-strokes, which ran on gas alone, or the Yamaha and Kawasaki models with oil injection. They were offered with three-speed shifts when Japanese bikes offered four or five speeds. They made lawn-mower-like sounds that did not appeal to the American cyclist in search of a muted roar.

The Europeans, if they had failed in the multimillion-dollar small-bike market, were not about to let pass the opportunity to stuff the coffers with American dollars provided by power-hungry colonials.

Though rumors ran wild concerning various Japanese big bores supposedly in the testing stage, the word was out that the Japanese were going to limit their motorcycle output to a maximum of 450 c.c. They were making money hand over fist with the small bikes that everyone was buying and did not really want to retool all their factories and put themselves in the displacement competition against their European counterparts.

The British, bless their souls, had already developed and marketed various fire breathers guaranteed to outstrip anything on the road . . . if you could stand it.

Birmingham Small Arms, an erstwhile armament manufacturer that put out the BSA and Triumph motorcycles, Norton-Villiers, which made the Norton Atlas, and Royal Enfield, manufacturers of the R.E. and, at one time, partner to the now-defunct Enfield-Indian Motorcycle Company, were all capable of building a perfect machine, but not particularly eager to, for the British cyclist, steeped in classicism, had found satisfaction straddling a belching, oil-leaking and vibrating monster.

The Bavarian Motor Works were still building BMWs, much as they had been building them for over twenty years, but BMWs were specialized pieces of machinery made for one type of rider—the road or touring freak. They had reputations of steady but not particularly good handling, steady but not astoundingly fast acceleration. And they looked funny, at least to the American way of seeing things: the two cylinders sticking transversely out of the engine were bound to get smashed if the bike fell over. The one-color choice (black) did little for their sales.

Changes, which had to come in order to survive, seemed to run against the grain, if not against the pocketbook.

The changes came. The British smoothed out their engines, padded the seats of their fire belchers, and tried, though they often failed, to cure their oil leaks.

The machines from England became a status symbol among riders, with the Triumph 650 c.c. models taking precedence over most imported models. Norton pushed a radically new concept in frames, the "Featherbed," designed to glue the motorcycle to the road, even during the tightest turns, and the later "Isolastic," which insured less vibrations. And all three major British companies resorted to the American style of advertising.

Loud claims of power vied for attention. Color photography displays abounded. There were contests and freebies given to bike buyers. Warranties were advertised. Accessories included, aftersale service promised, regular tune-ups offered. Free gas. Free helmets. Free jacket patches, passes for races, dates, driving lessons, insurance advice . . .

By the late 1960s, a full-scale advertising war bloodied the pages of most national magazines (*Playboy, Life,* etc.,) with ad copy ranging the full gamut of claims.

Honda boasted knowledge and power coupled with a score of international-race results. Yamaha, rather modestly, simply said "It's a Better Machine," while Kawasaki hired race-car driver Parnelli Jones and sat him atop an Avenger 350 c.c., all the while subtly asking the reader, "Are You the Kawasaki Kind?" Suzuki put out a series of machines that strangely resembled early Hondas and claimed the added power was "The Next Logical Step." Bridgestone exaggeratedly claimed "unequalled performance with years ahead styling" but showed up instead with strange pieces of machinery already outdated by the time they hit the market.

It was enough to confuse the buyers. One issue of *Motorcyclist* magazine

Evel Knievel, daredevil flesh and blood hero on his Harley-Davidson XR-750. A wheelie for the fans.

carried two full-page ads stating that both Norton and Ducati had won the Daytona and Sebring races. They did, of course, but in different classes. This was in smaller print.

Birmingham Small Arms (BSA) and Norton discovered that sex could sell motorcycles. Scantily dressed women lounged on top of, in front of, and behind sparkling red BSAs. The circle had just about made a full turn, the motorcycles were once again associated with the forbidden.

This caused a slight uproar among readers of motorcycle magazines. One incensed subscriber to *Cycle* wrote an anonymous letter:

> How about some responsibility in advertising. Take back your lousy nude with the ink job. Don't want trash in my cycle books. We buy motorcycles, not prostitutes—which you are selling is hard to tell.

Another decried the implicit danger of nudity in bike magazines and bemoaned the fact that he now had to censor his *Cycle* magazine before letting his kids have it. *Cycle* magazine espoused what can only be called a Playboy philosophy, castigating the author of the letter, and saying, "The kind of evil you see exists only in the eye of the beholder . . ."

Motorcycle manufacturers had, in fact, realized what disseminators of everything from Band-Aids to hair spray had long ago seen and applied—Naked Women Sell. And the motorcycle regained its standing as a sex object. But even then, the advertising was tame compared to what was to come. Norton, BMW, Triumph, all made sexual allusions in their advertising, but there was no overt implication. No motorcycle manufacturer went as far as to say that the purchase of his product would get the girl into your bed. It might get you close to her, but you took it from there.

Less than three years later, several motorcycle accessory companies were sending out catalogues displaying two-page nudes with more than beckoning smiles and Yamaha had injected religion in its ads by featuring Father Dale Peterka, Associate Pastor of Our Lady of Lourdes Catholic Church in Cincinnati, Ohio, who swore in a two-page foldout that he had logged 7,500 on his Yamaha without one blessed thing going wrong.

It was a long, long way from the early Excelsior and Brough Superior ads portraying dashing young men on bicycle-like machines with "round torpedo gas tanks and detachable footrests."

2

People, Angels, and Racing Saints

The motorcycle revolution that has in the past ten years swept the land is undoubtedly one of the most egalitarian movements to strike. It literally knows no racial, religious, or economic bias, though it is primarily centered around the middle and lower-middle class. Blacks, Jews, atheists, Mexican-Americans, and Catholics ride, race, and occasionally raise hell just as spontaneously as their WASP neighbors. The only party that has so far chosen to abstain is the women's faction, and there the choice has not been dictated but is entirely voluntary, perhaps for good reason. For all the shiny candy-appled-and-chromed paint jobs appearing on the market, motorcycles are still conceived with the man in mind. Their very design is centered around the male apparel, if not the male anatomy, and no one has yet attempted to build the true woman's motorcycle. The early open frame designs espoused by Honda, Yamaha, Suzuki, and a host of smaller companies can and often are ridden by women, but the limited size of the engine (a maximum of 90 c.c.) render them unable to reach speeds attained by larger motorcycles. These small machines, by their very configuration, are closer to the mo-ped and motor scooters made in Europe than they are to motorcycles. Other

The compactness and agility of motorcycles is being rediscovered. An increasing number of large and small firms are hiring motorcycle messengers who can cut down delivery time. BMWs are popular machines for such work.

reasons, perhaps, can be found in the fact that helmets have a tendency to ruin hairdos while leathers are highly uncomplimentary to most female figures. And motorcycles, after all, are simply not elegant. What can be considered slightly raunchy and possibly sexy for a man will not do much for a woman with the exception of labeling her a sexual deviant, a "butch," a "dyke," a "lez." If male motorcyclists are plagued by homosexual myths, the woman-bikers' social standing is infinitely lower, a fact that can be proven if one considers basic statistics:

Less than 5 percent of the riders are women and though there are some notable exceptions—the Desert Daisies and the Motor Maids—it's still, as far as most bikers are concerned, a man's world.

A *Cycle* magazine survey taken in October, 1970, said the average rider who read the magazine was 25.7 years old, earned $11,708 annually, and had a 55 percent chance of being a white-collar businessman. Of these businessmen, 41 percent were executives, managers or professional, all of which is a fairly long step from the average-man's idea of riders being leather-jacketed ruffians. There are some, but they're damned few and far between

Evel wows 'em at the Kansas State Fair. A lot of money, a lot of broken bones, metal pins, and a movie on his life have made him one of the last of the great stuntmen.

when compared to the majority, and not too popular even among their fellow cyclists.

The original cyclists were fairly individualistic souls. They had to be. They looked upon motorcycles not as virility-enhancing symbols but rather as swift, noisy, and sometimes uncomfortable vehicles that restored the almost pioneering thrill of reaching a destination. And, after all, why not? Psychological implications were not bandied about as freely then as they are now, and if bikers were considered just a mite strange, a wee bit out of the ordinary to a nation that still viewed speed and overmobility as the precursor of changing times, at least their sexual life was not openly debated by backyard and armchair experts. The original outlook has changed somewhat since then, and more than a few riders presently stride their machines in order to pull up failing *machismo* and low popularity quotients. In this respect, and many others, the multimillion-dollar advertising campaigns have paid off. Motorcycles have been put roughly on the same level as underarm deodorants and do-it-yourself daily Aikido courses. Own one and you're a man, regardless of your ability to ride it. Bikes are now being peddled as equalizers, a step short of the sawed-off shotgun and a step past the Charles-Atlas-barbell-instruction books. A 110-pound weakling on a Harley 1,200 c.c. will look fairly impressive, and chances are no one will mess with him, at least not while he's on his machine. The non-biking population has applied to both a motorcycle and its rider the age-old formula of association: if the bike is big, so, probably, is its owner. The larger the bike, the fiercer the rider, and vice versa . . . Off the Harley, it's another matter entirely, as some luckless riders have discovered much to their dismay.

Speed and power have been equated with strength and manliness, as if sheer horsepower were the equivalent of bulging muscles and flat stomachs. The nature and form of the advertisements now displayed prominently are not accidental. Rather, they're calculated, well-planned, and superbly executed maneuvers exploiting man's greatest insecurities—weakness and impotence.

They do wondrously well. For every ten motorcycles sold, one is probably delivered to a rather sorry individual seeking motorized magic, in sore need of moral and physical bolstering to override an imagined or real handicap. The best example of this phenomenon, and the one that has become *the* example, is Marlon Brando's portrayal of Johnny in *The Wild One*.

Johnny—no last name is necessary—is a man-child beset by problems with which he cannot cope. He mumbles, he stutters. He says "duh" and "uh" too often. What to his cohort baddies passes off as manliness is actually a deep-seated form of insecurity.

He is obviously uneducated, an unexciting blue-collar worker whose only redemption is his cycle. But on the machine, he's transformed into a god, a graceful one at that, a Clark Kent turned Superman, devoid of humanity's frailties, an elemental force that brooks no resistance. Johnny can and does, on at least two occasions, get the crap beat out of him, but that's part of his life. He is, at best, a physical creature who can hand out and take physical punishment with equal verve, and even make wise cracks while his head is being knocked about like a hockey puck. But when resistance of another type, be it emotional or mental, is met in the form of the sheriff's daughter—whose power is subtly more influential than the Triumph twin—Johnny crumbles and again turns mortal, deserted by the deities that propelled him.

And a jump for the money . . .

Touring in all-American style. The Harley-Davidson Electra Glide motorcycle, courtesy Milwaukee. Called Milwaukee iron by some, garbage wagon by others and "the best motorcycle made" by die-hard fans, the Electra Glide is the United States' and the world's largest mass-produced motorcycle.

If some riders are taken in by the advertisers' claims, the great majority is not.

Bikers, it seems, are more realistic than ad-men, a fact that to this day, advertising agencies refuse to believe. The machines sold are in reality largely purchased as deterrents to nine-to-five boredom in gray offices manned by grayer people. They give the paper-pusher the sought-for opportunity to become something other than what he really is.

The accountant becomes Steve McQueen in *The Great Escape*, Peter Fonda in *Easy Rider*. The older riders see them as a link to youth, the youths consider them insurance against a paper-pushing future, old age, and infirmity. Everyone can ride. Everyone can forget himself, forget his lackluster present. The motorcycle is a wonderful dream machine.

There are basically three types of riders, if one might exclude the rather small segment of motorcycle people, professional racers, delivery men, testers, and cops who make their livelihood aboard cycles.

The majority of riders are already car owners before they purchase their machines and seek motorcycles as a joint answer to high motoring fees, gasoline costs, and traffic jams. Others purchase machines strictly as recreational vehicles that they can pound into the dirt on weekends while maintaining their status as automobile drivers during the week. Some purchase bikes because the cycles come closer to the Aston Martin they'll never be able to afford than an MGB or TR-4 ever will. These riders, though a varied lot, often seek companionship by forming or joining a riding club.

There are thousands of clubs in North America, all designed for and by riders for the primary purpose of furthering their enjoyment. Virtually every major motorcycle make that is or has been manufactured has its own little group of *aficionados* who ride together, exchange information, and, as a rule, bask in the glory and admiration of their machine over all other brands. There are restorers' clubs, touring clubs, kids' clubs and old people's clubs, racing clubs, clubs for girls and women, and mechanics clubs . . .

The formation of riding clubs can be traced back to the very dawn of motorcycling when riders discovered it can be more fun to go double or triple than single. The element of safety entered the picture when motorcycles were so unreliable that they were almost certain to break down. Having another rider along would provide help and if nothing else a means of transportation back to the garage. Another factor dictated that it was far safer to ride in numbers to discourage the pranks that motorists often practiced in rather bad taste. Noncyclists were still into cowboy-and-Indian games, and chasing a hapless cyclist off the road and into the cornfields was considered the epitome of Sunday-afternoon amusement. Chasing two machines into a ditch was a bit harder, as motorcyclists were thought to act much like wolves, protecting their mates. Trying to get a dozen machines off the road was downright dangerous. *Ergo*, ride in numbers.

As the clubs multiplied, they started diverging into special-interest groups, which in turn opened chapters around the country, set up a code of rules and organizations, and fostered even smaller splinter groups. California again led the trend, simply because the weather, the riding terrain, and availability of machines were all far better than in any other state. The first clubs, contrary to many opinions, were not outlaws at all. They made noise and looked imposing, maybe even scary, but did not go out of their way to cause trouble. Rather, they went to great lengths to avoid it. But trouble seemed to manifest itself too often for the tastes of many who considered the machines and their riders far too wild and woolly in an era trying to be sophisticated. Incidents of drunkenness were not common but not rare enough to avoid certain unsightly scenes. The cyclists were far too boisterous to please small towners and too cliquish for the bigger cities, and even if the average rider did not, and still does not, get all that much pleasure from exasperating others, the simple fact that he is more on display and more conscious of his vulnerability has helped foster the very reputation that he seeks to avoid. Be that as it may, the aura surrounding motorcycles was attached to clubs, for what applied to a lone rider applied in spades to a bunch of riders. What originally were small groups of people interested in furthering their sport against too-often-discriminatory forms of shotgun justice soon became the much touted enemy of all that was civilized. The local cop was wary of one cycle, suspicious of two, and scared of three. And fright has often ended disastrously, fostering a sort of blindness that groups elements of a different sort without the least variation, preferring to stuff everything in one bag and let it go at that.

The psychological aspect of the motorcyclist's own reputation entered too. What one cyclist could not do, five could, and with impunity. There's something almost Satanic about a score of machines being ridden through a town or down the highway, a sheer feeling of unadulterated power strong enough to rival sex. Cyclists, particularly in a bunch, look so damned superior astride their machines, so utterly unreachable that their appearance alone is enough to make the average motorist see red.

Sheltered by the sheet-iron carcass separating him from the outside world, a car driver is apt to feel that bikers are just a bit too damned superior, and start playing tag with them, a dangerous sport not only for the bikers but also for the driver's health and automobile. Nothing is more infuriating than heading down a road at a steady sixty only to realize that a bare six inches behind your rear wheel is an automobile with a smirking driver intent on playing what he supposes is a good practical joke. Many a car's fenders and hoods have suffered from the well-aimed kicks of generally pacific bikers whose patience has reached an end . . .

The clubs grew, until one central club was needed to serve as a hub to

The Compleat Tourer I, Ben Harroll, Ambassador E. & P. of the International Four Owner's Association. Harroll rides a Honda 750 c.c. Four and traveled the length and breadth of the States promoting both his Association and the sport. His bike's fairings make him almost totally self-contained.

The Compleat Tourer II. Gentle Ben's nooks and crannies have been used intelligently. Harroll's ready for a year-long trip.

all others, coordinating sports events, meets, making rules, and setting guidelines.

The American Motorcycling Association was formed in 1924 to promote the sport of motorcycling. Located in Ohio, it obtained its major support from the American motorcycle manufacturer, Harley-Davidson. The AMA's association with the company was eventually to damage its influence, particularly during the Japanese-European invasion, which saw Harley-Davidson sales remain constant while everyone else's was growing by leaps and bounds. Until quite recently, the AMA was considered as little more than one of Harley-Davidson's advertising branches, by and large uninterested in the many problems facing the everyday riders and racers. The past two or three years have seen many changes within the AMA's organization, necessary changes encompassing public and legislative relations, the broadcast of safety-oriented television and radio programs, motorcycle-driving education, and the organization of a junior AMA for under-sixteen-year-old riders. The AMA also put out one of the best all-time-worst recordings entitled *Motorcycle Man,* which each and every rider should own if only to know what he should represent.

With approximately 200,000 members, the AMA is by far the nation's number one club, both in size and range of interest. Major races are held under AMA banners and according to AMA rules. They are won by AMA racers and refereed by AMA officials. The association has hired two full-time lobbyists to wear thin the carpets of the nation's Capitol and hopefully stem the tide of antimotorcycling laws now being legislated.

The AMA's effect on American motorcycling has been beneficial, even if one is tempted to consider their policy occasionally as slightly backward. It has concerned itself with the good of the sport and, more importantly, with its growth. There are now "Junior" AMA clubs, which cater, in particular, to minibike owners and stress safety above all things. The AMA's public-relations department churns out releases that emphasize motorcycling as an all-American sport. The association puts on shows and projects films, publishes a very slick and well-written monthly journal, and keeps racers and riders in touch with current motorcycling events.

And through all these activities, the AMA has waged a full war against the dreaded one percenters, gangs as opposed to clubs, doers of evil deeds, and tarnishers of good reputations.

Hell's Angels, Pagans, Rattlers, Satan's Slaves, Chicago Outlaws, and an

The Jersey Devils, a group from Atlantic City. The shot, taken in 1965, reflects the early customizing scene. Harleys were still full-dressed, and British bikes sported "ape hangers," tall handlebars, which later were outlawed in many states. Leather was in.

occasional lone rider with a No Club patch on his back or an obscenity stenciled on denim with Magic Marker. The all-American hooligans, exotic names bespeaking evil. Visions of outrageous machines preceded and followed by the smell of grease and sweat, gasoline and blood. Visions of violence and rapes, obscenities committed, unpunished, in public; acts against nature with subtle tendencies of homosexuality and leather fetishes. The heavy, the rebel, but not in the accepted sense of the Robin Hood word, the dreg of society, so low even other cyclists will not associate with him.

The motorcycle outlaw has made his mark in the United States, a mark that has made the wealth and joy of some, a mark which definitely shows a perverted sense of romanticism desperately trying to associate violence and ignorance with Count of Monte Cristo-ish valor. The outlaw gangs are followed and sought out with a sick fascination by an entire population in search of vicarious kicks and an almost self-destructive wish to see if they're really as mean as everyone says they are, tempered by a certainty that they aren't, not really, they couldn't be.

They are. The American society has nurtured a false image of the outlaw, as virtually every society has, possibly as a reminder of better and simpler things, more likely as an obscure form of wish fulfillment. Sonny Barger, president of the Hell's Angels, once stated that deep down, most men wished they could ride motorcycles and be as mean as the gang members are, and sad to say, he's probably right. The outlaws are an almost sacred part of popular history. They have escaped the censorship of time and have assumed a rightful place next to the fearless sheriff of Tucson Junction. Billy the Kid didn't really kill anyone, and neither did Ma Barker. Robin Hood is alive and well in New York City, John Dillinger and Al Capone were for a time the example to be followed if one was in search of quick and effortless money and fame.

Lawlessness has always attracted the masses unable to become renegades and unwilling to live up to the legends they created. The motorcycle gangs have followed the deification of other violent groups, and the only difference is one of time. It's really difficult to envisage that right here in the golden land, right here where television, 3-D movies, McDonald's, and root beer were invented, a group of downright ornery bastards could take root and grow to be pop symbols, their everyday actions and words taken quite seriously, their opinions debated by the press and media, their feats enlarged and legendary scarcely after completion, their threats enough to mobilize police forces statewide and bring tourists from miles around.

The motorcycle gangs stand alone both in their existence and reputation, much more respectable than the street gangs of yore and more enjoyable (and profitable) than their ancestors the hot rodders.

The first honest to goodness cycle meanies to gain fame were riders who took the unlikely name of Booze Fighters in the mid-1940s and, in 1947, with the aid of AMA members participating in the Association's annual Gypsy tour, started the Hollister riots, which eventually influenced the filming of *The Wild One*. It's doubtful that any of the original Booze Fighters still wear outlaw colors, but their offspring, a loosely knit club which called

itself the Market Street Commandos, can lay claim to becoming the second, and most important, chartered Hell's Angels motor cycle club.

Birney Jarvis, a reporter for the San Francisco *Chronicle*, in an article for *Male* magazine, described the actual metamorphosis from Commando to Angel:

One hot summer day in 1954, a swarthily handsome devil, sporting a pointed beard and derby, broadslid his Harley-Davidson to a screeching halt at a motorcycle hangout in San Francisco.

His faded blue Levis jacket, the sleeves roughly hacked off with a knife, was emblazoned with the leering, winged death's head that has become so well known to California lawmen.

You could see the sweat-stained armpits of his checkered shirt as he wrestled the four-foot-high handlebars into position. With a flick of his wrist he blasted the afternoon quiet of a Sunday on Market Street.

He laid his bike over on the kickstand, polished the glistening chrome of his "XA" spring forks—four inches longer than stock—with a ragged handkerchief. He looked around him, nonchalantly wiping his greasy hands on his oil-crusted jeans.

This was Rocky. Nobody cared what his last name was because he was "classical" and he was a Hell's Angel from down Berdoo way.

Thirty cyclists with polished boots and neatly barbered hair had watched his arrival, not without suspicion because he was, at that time, a stranger and all of them had been riding pals for a long time. The welcoming committee was prime for membership in the Hell's Angels. Although completely square compared to the latter-day Angels, the street corner gang had had constant brushes with the law . . . Rocky was elected president of the new branch of the Hell's Angels because he could really ride and because he had style.

"He could spin donuts on that hog with his feet on the pegs, and man, he was a wiggy cat," a member of the Angels recalled. The cyclists found a seamstress who could duplicate Rocky's sinister emblem and it wasn't long before nearly 40 Angels were roaring out of San Francisco. The neat "Hell's Angels-Frisco" surrounding the grinning skull with wings cost $7.50 and was ordinarily sewn on a Levis jacket. The white background of the red lettering soon became spotted with grime—and blood—from the many barroom battles that ensued.

From the Angels sprouted a number of smaller offspring, clubs that have amassed a certain amount of fame and who still hope, some day, to achieve the status of their California fathers.

An estimated two hundred and fifty members of the Hell's Angels motorcycle club are escorted by San Diego police to the funeral of their vice president, Andrew Horn. Horn was killed in June, 1970, in a gunbattle with a rival motorcycle club.

Few clubs have garnered the notoriety of the Hell's Angels Motorcycle Club of California. Their "runs" are followed on nationwide TV, preempting "I Love Lucy" and even "Wide World of Sports." They are mobbed by applicants and charter seekers wanting to establish Hell's Angels franchises from Alaska to Florida. They are the subject of an official report by the California state-attorney's office, a report, which, incidentally, was quoted by major newspapers and proved to be largely erroneous. They inspired countless cheap paperbacks and one excellent book written by Hunter Thompson, now of *Rolling Stone* magazine. They are the heroes of many movies, the inspiration of miles of newsprint, the idols of uncounted young men who junked their Yamahas and Hondas to sink their college money into a full-fledged California chopper. The Angels' rise to fame is directly responsible for the popularity of the chopper and for the creation of a multimillion-dollar accessories industry, which changes the Harley-Davidson motorcycles from gross hunks of steel and chrome to outrageous hunks of steel and chrome. Angel's hirsute faces have graced the cover of the now defunct *Saturday Evening Post*. They've been written up in *Time* and *Newsweek*, were the subject of an off-Broadway rock opera, the police's best enemies, Ken Kesey's and Allen Ginsburg's one-time favorite friends, the protectors and eventual assaulters of the early flower and antiwar folks. . . . According to Mexican border guards, they are undoubtedly the biggest dope smugglers now operating, a hard claim to substantiate, even if every Harley-Davidson gas tank in California were filled with grass. They are, in short, the victims of the very reputation they strove for, and at this point, really don't know how to handle.

The Angels are a hassled group. They've been forced to disband more than one chapter; fourteen of their members in Cleveland, Ohio, recently were found guilty of manslaughter; others are in jail; some are strung out on various drugs; some have become cops. It wasn't always that way, and, in fact, there was, once upon a time, a reform movement sweeping the ranks.

Becoming, much to their surprise, the darlings of the media, the Angels and later other gangs decided one day that the heat was too great and tried to go straight, if only to get the cops off their backs. The method chosen was fraught in the very cloak of diplomacy. They would reform and become good guys. The movement, unfortunately, was to be short-lived. The proposed idea was that the bikers become white knights of the road, much like their earlier hot-rodding brothers in the fifties, and aid stranded motorists by changing flat tires, starting stalled cars, and being general all-around nice people. The movement was off to a rousing good start, and the club members had hundreds of little white engraved calling cards made saying "You have just been helped by Big Mother of the Hell's Angels Motorcycle Club, Please Drive Safely." They hit the roads and freeways, avidly searching for broken-down motorists like a horde of Saint Francises looking for battered birds. Once such a motorist was found, perplexed, with motor steaming in the hot California sun, they'd stop, en masse, carefully park their chopped hogs on the shoulder of the road, unload monkey wrench, tire irons, and all the accouterment of the roadside mechanic, and amble over to the lucky driver in need of their ministration. The driver would as a rule turn sheet-white and remember horrible newspaper tales of rapes and torture by the very hoodlums who were now approaching him with instruments of violence tightly clenched in their greasy fists. At this point, the motorist would react in one of three ways. He'd abandon his car and run down the highway screaming like a maniac or he'd jump into his car, lock the doors, roll up the windows, and sit on the horn. Or worse, he'd initiate an attack, bolstered by all the aikido and karate lessons of the Friday Night Self-Defense Club, and invariably get spread all over the pavement, thereby, once again, worsening the reputation of his would-be saviours. The Angels would at first make sounds of friendship, but it was often hard to believe that a six-foot-six pierced-eared wildman bedecked in swastikas, smelling like an outhouse, waving a monkey wrench, and looking as if he would simply love to cleave your head in two could actually be all that friendly.

Before his untimely and fatal motorcycle jump from Key Bridge into the Potomac River, Little Jesus, a member of the East Coast Pagans Motorcycle Club, a would-be Hell's Angel group that has succeeded better than most clubs, recounted the day the club stopped to help a stranded motorist on the Washington Beltway. The man, seeing a horde of ruffians approaching him, jumped into the trunk of his car and pulled the lid shut as insurance against bodily harm that might befall him. The Pagans, taken aback by this show of ingratitude, philosophically shrugged it off and called a state policeman—a first in motorcycle-gang history—telling him simply that some dude was locked in the trunk of a car and that someone should get him out before he suffocated. They were hard-pressed to explain how the man got there in the first place. The man, once rescued, ranted about being threatened. The Pagans shook their heads sadly and decided to junk the

Love in America: The Satan's Few, a small club in Maryland, celebrate the marriage of Evel to Loser. The vows were pronounced by ex-member Preacher, an ordained member of the Universal Life Church.

Death in America: The Pagans, largest "outlaw" club in the East Coast, attend the outdoor funeral of one of their members. Also in attendance were various representatives of other groups such as the Satan's Few, the D.C. Phantoms, and the Vagabondos.

entire program, giving up good deeds and using the engraved cards solely among themselves and other clubs.

The motorcycle gangs, for all their ruthlessness and seeming asociality, are actually based on a stringent code of ethics mindful of Marine Corps boot camp. The basic rules are set and rigid, and one must unquestioningly comply. There's little room for personal ideas and ambitions. Though monthly meetings are held to clarify certain regulations and admit or reject a potential new member, the basic credo governing a gang's actions can never be debated. A member who does not, for personal reasons, wish to join in certain facets of the merrymaking will be dismissed summarily, and often violently. The d'Artagnan philosophy has been bastardized from all for one and one for all "to all on one." Attacks against a member of the club will warrant reprisals by all. Money is to be shared, as are club women, dope, liquor, and motorcycle parts. The only personal belongings allowed by the charter rules are two: a man's motorcycle and his colors, which he may not wash. Outsiders are frowned upon, as are strong friendships and relationships outside the club.

One of the greatest myths concerning motorcycle gangs is based around the thought that many gang members are leather-fetishistic, homosexually bent weirdos with much talk and little action. Anyone who has faced a gang in a barroom brawl or street fight is bound to quickly review his opinion. They're for real, and if some do indulge in rather strange sex rites, homosexuality is not the issue. Kicks are; incongruousness and repulsiveness are carefully cultivated fashions made to rip straighter minds apart, made to test manhood versus weak stomachs.

The future of the motorcycle gangs is hazy. Though they are on the upsurge now, chances are their popularity will diminish before long. In a highly technical world, gang members are totally hopeless individuals, incapable of bending or learning, unwilling to become joiners, yet perfectly lucid when it comes to their own roles, or lack of them. Customizing genius Ed Roth once called them modern-day Robin Hoods and attempted to sell Hell's Angels T-shirts. The Angels warned that anyone caught wearing the T-shirt would have it ripped off his back. Their answer to Ed Roth's compliment was an unchivalrous four-letter word.

The Angels' popularity, at least among the younger long-haired generation, has been on the wane ever since the Altamont fiasco, for, along with other atrocious deeds, the California bikers can now be held responsible for the death of the Woodstock nation.

During a 1970 free concert in Altamont, California, Mick Jagger, of the British Rolling Stones rock group, had the disastrous idea of inviting the Angels to guard the stage against the fierce teeny-boppers and fans. The reward for this favor was to be as much beer as the bikers could drink. The Angels, in a manner that would make riot cops proud, made outstanding bodyguards, blithely tossing people off the stage and into the crowds, subduing the hardier ones with sawed-off and leaded pool cues. Then, in front of some thirty cameras filming the rock festival, and before the horrified eyes of thousands of music freaks, the gang proceeded to beat and stab to death a young black man suspected of pointing a gun at the stage.

It was the last straw. Americans can tolerate most anything, and are more than willing to forgive and forget, but murder, right there smack dab in the middle of all the good peace, love, and dope vibes, was just too much to handle. The Angels, though in the end acquitted in court, could no longer be considered one of the lost tribes. The long hairs, as one, turned their back sorrowfully on their motorcycled brothers and wrote them off the ledger of people-to-get-tight-with.

The gang accepted the rejection and once again closed their ranks. After all, they reasoned, they hadn't really wanted to get into this scene in the first place. Sure, the freaks were fun, but it was Kesey who had first invited them to those strange parties at his estate, and after awhile, it was the Angels who were supplying the dope when times were hard. There had been good times, but this turn around just proved a basic Angel point: stick with your brothers, don't go looking for friends; anyone not wearing the colors is a potential enemy; the brother Angels must tighten up, get their organization together and stop messing around with the people whose heads are into so much dope that they can't think straight.

The motorcycle gangs will vanish, if only because they'll be overrun by straighter clubs, because the little use the world presently finds for them—their entertainment value—will soon disappear, perhaps making way for more modern gangs, snowmobilers or renegade helicopter pilots. Legally, their prolonged existence is in doubt. If they aren't run off the road by irate state troopers, their customized Harley-Davidson motorcycles might very well be legislated to look like Honda 175s. Their demise may be even more unromantic, and, twenty years in the future, a bunch of middle-aged beer-bellied man aboard factory-built choppers will reminisce of the good old days when they, at least, were individuals. And if the gangs do not, by some natural process, eliminate themselves totally, the police forces of various states will do it for them, probably with a thankful and possibly slightly sadistic grin.

In California, the Hell's Angels, or what is left of the few not recently busted for murder, tax evasion, dope, rape, and other illegal pastimes, have all gone underground. Top Angel Sonny Barger lingers in jail. A man riding a chop with Angel colors is asking for it, and few straights are there to protect his equal rights. He'll be harassed, checked, followed, lured, and eventually arrested on one ground or another. The state, it seems, has finally decided to cure itself of its cancer. The other, smaller gangs, seeing the plight of their more famous cohorts, are lying low, and the sound of two strokes is now more common than the rumble of a modified Harley.

If motorcycle gangs are presently in the public eye, another group of bikers, a far more important and interesting group both in outlook and number, seems to be heading for public recognition.

One out of four motorcycle owners in the United States races his machine, mostly on a novice or amateur level, strictly for the enjoyment of the sport. Racers, like gang members, are a breed unto themselves. There is no money involved in amateur racing, just trophies and the sheer excitement generated by most sports that involve speed and handling. The racers put virtually anything on the track, from small European and Japanese 50 c.c. machines with multiple gears and staccato exhausts on the smooth banks of a road race to huge multicylinder four-strokes, which pound themselves to bits and pieces on drag races and hill climbs.

Two movies, *Little Halsey and Big Fauss* and *On Any Sunday*, have illustrated the racers' lives. *On Any Sunday* was nominated for an Academy Award for its portrayal of the various races attended every Sunday by a generally all-American cross section of the population, but it failed to show the before and after effect that losing or winning can have, the entire passion that some racers feel, and, occasionally, the nail-biting sheer frustrations involved with racing.

When you wake up in the middle of the night before a race, your stomach is tight, and before you come to the full realization of who you are and where you are, your brain will try to remember what you might have overlooked while readying your bike, because there are so many things that can go wrong, so many ridiculous engine failures that can leave you coasting to a stop while the rest of the pack blithely sails past, feet out and

Amateur racing has blossomed into a widely practiced sport, both on the East and West Coast. Dirt racing, since it's far cheaper than asphalt, has thousands of fans. Most dirt racers prefer middle-sized two-stroke machines with wide pulling bands and high torque.

leaning way over, drowning you in a wave of buzzing and rasping cacophony, choking you in blue exhaust smoke reeking of oil and gas and leathery sweat and burning rubber, and all those things that pass through your head in that instant between sleep and wakefulness are far more important than who and where you are.

So it's not unusual at all, the night before a race, to see the riders who can't afford a motel room come out of their vans and campers and pick-up trucks at two or three in the morning, with swollen faces and grimy fingernails from the day before, lugging wrenches and ratchets and spare plugs to their machines.

Because a lot of them can't sleep if it's a big race, or an important race, or a first race. So they come back to the brightly painted machines they've left just a few hours earlier and check everything again, the adjustments and tensions and gaps and jet sizes and tire cuts, and they'll fiddle with the timing, getting it just so, and still not be totally satisfied, still be prey to the little gnawing worry in the back of the head. If sleep is still too elusive, and rest at this point seems hopeless, they'll congregate around the van of one man who might have a rheostat and some sour instant coffee with instant cream or an extra six pack of beer, and they'll talk, just talk, exchanging information that they've probably exchanged before. It kills the time in the middle of the night, the time until those first preliminary heats are run, the very heats that might make the 150 traveled miles a waste of time. And one will leave, another will come, until only two or three are left, verbally tearing down an engine or a front end and rebuilding it, matching stories and exaggerations and myths created just during the last race when So-and-So wiped out while in first place and pushed his bike, broken ankle and all, all the way to the checkered flag one hundred yards away. And some will discuss strategy with a depth of knowledge that might impress a chess master, because strategy is as important to the racers as the machines they are riding.

One school will hang slightly back on the line when the starting flag is down, and another group will go gung ho, trying to beat the pack, regardless of all the books and fine how-to articles in glossy motorcycle magazines. Some say if you hang back just a bit, the untried novices with brand-new machines and clean number plates will knock themselves right out of the race, riding into one another in the excitement of it all, scratching the expensive new Bates leathers. Others say, yes, sure, it works if you've got a big field of first timers whose throttle hands are just a bit too trembly, too excited, but when it happens, how do you get past the tangle of arms, legs, wheels, spokes, and bent-up gear-shift levers? The very best thing to do, in almost all occasions, is to plow ahead, before the starter's flag has even reached the height of its swing, throttle quickly without making the novice's mistake of impressively pulling your front wheel into the air, wowing the crowds and losing time. There's less dust that way too, fewer people to pass later, less chances to take.

Eliminations start at 8:00 A.M., and the great majority of the riders have already donned part of their racing outfit at that time. The riders' meeting is the same usual drivel, with a bored AMA official telling them: you can't pass here or there, watch your elbows, you're all good boys and remember that you're representing American motorcycling, so keep it clean and good-natured.

The assortment of wives, girl friends, sons, daughters, fathers, and spectators arrive with picnic hampers and beers and six packs of Seven-Up. There are usually a couple of kids hustling programs with a smiling picture of Gary Nixon on the cover, and there's a dilapidated hot-dog and warm-Coke stand. Sometimes, the racers feel this is closer to a gladiator fight than a race. A lot of people come to see the blood, regardless of what they or the promoters say. The ambulance discreetly parked near the pits and near enough to the track to make it there in a hurry isn't hired just for looks.

In the pits, people are scurrying around trying to mooch a spare plug or quart of oil or tire or advice.

The racers line up for the start. Some people have called them weekend gun fighters because once they're up on the line, the ones who know what they're doing don't waver. They've already made all the mistakes they can make, in many races before this one, and now the only part of them that moves is the wrist, trying to keep the machine clean, right near the small power line that wavers on the tachometer. The bikes make sounds that rise and fall in discordant crescendos. The racers don't blink; in the blink of an eye, the flag can fall, and they might be left behind. The start of a race is the tensest moment, and when that flag falls, they're off, and the knot in the stomach dissolves for lack of attention. During the race, the tension diminishes among the riders, even if it increases in the audience. It's deadly to be too nervous. The right formula is physical looseness and mental awareness, a capability of being able to gauge angles and turns and speeds while going eighty or ninety miles per hour—a careful application of instant, almost instinctive know-how: who to pass, where, when. As the race winds on, the riders come to know the circuit a bit better, every lap adding to that ability to sense the next curve before it comes. They can anticipate the jumps, the potholes, and ruts, and only the inexperienced are still knotted up. And the inexperienced invariably lose to a calmer man. The riders are in their elements. The race is the culmination of a week's worry, a week's anticipation, endless hours of preparation, and if the bike holds up and doesn't crap out like so many do, the burden is all on the rider, his strength and weakness, his physical stamina and ability to take the necessary jars and bumps.

There are fewer machines on the track now. Some have wiped out in the sheer joy of finally getting to the track. Some bikes have died, in spite of the broken fingernails and skinned knuckles. They die with coughs and sputters and a hiss of blue smoke, making sounds like a bathtub drain sucking in the last of the water. The spark plug fouled or the gas line clogged or something more intricate and more imponderable happened, a loose wire way down deep in the wiring harness, a hairline crack that spread and lunched an engine.

Toward the end, a few of the more seasoned racers are up front, and the tenseness comes back, but now it's a calculated tenseness, a nervousness tempered by the knowledge of what they're up against. By the last lap, the racers no longer need conserve any energy, and battle for first, second, and third. The battle for first is the one watched by the audience, but enough difference exists between third and fourth to make that fight interesting, and by the time the checkered flag falls some of the racers are too tired to give much of a damn about anything except sitting down on something immobile for a change and trying to regain the pound or so they lost in sweat during the race. Some are disgusted, both by their machines and by themselves. Some rail against unfair decisions, bad courses, and ignorant promoters. Some are comforted, others lean against their machines with a small bubble of solitude separating them from the crowd. Some clean and drain their cycles, trying to figure out what went wrong when it did, and why.

And all will be back for next week's race, a little bit more wary of the curve, a shade more reserved with their throttle.

The weekend people, racers, club riders, outlaws, renegades, and loners all have in common membership to an overwhelmingly male club. The women in motorcycling are rare, exceedingly so. There are, however, a few organizations for women riders and racers. In the West, the Desert Daisies give male racers a certain amount of well-deserved grief. And all over the United States, with charters in virtually every state, the Motor Maids give motorcycling a new dimension.

Comprised solely of women, who as a rule ride large BMWs or Harley Glides, the MMs squash lacquered hair beneath monogrammed helmets, don snappy uniforms, and take the roads, often husbandless, in the best traditions attributed to pioneering females. Middle America on two wheels, last outpost of sacred womanhood in a nation ravaged and belabored by female liberators and practitioners of planned parenthood, the Motor Maids hang on to the traditional ways of life; their members are never spoken of as women; they're referred to, in the monthly AMA news, as "Girls," all frills, bows, and laces. The monthly reports are mindful of a time gone by, as are the Maids themselves, a time of simplicity unhampered by long-hairs, cultural revolutions, dope, campus rebels, and draft dodgers. Motorcycles have reached a level of social acceptability, which, in view of their general reputation, borders on the very ridiculous. Who can possibly accuse a Motor Maid

A chapter of the Motor Maids at Daytona, 1971. Bringing motorcycling to the mom-and-apple-pie level, some of the better people who've dulled the bad-guy image.

grandmother of being a black-jacketed ruffian, and what violence can be expected from people who meet monthly in suburban homes laden with Sears furniture to share coffee and cake and chuckle quietly over the antics of Carrie and Bud's trip to Hawaii last fall?

What the AMA, the Motorcycle Industry Council, the wails of thousands of riders, the concerted wealths of the ten biggest motorcycle manufacturers aided by the greatest of Madison Avenue's ad agencies might never hope to accomplish, the Motor Maids might very well achieve: that is, to make motorcycling as acceptable as a quilting bee and innocuous as a taffy pull or apple bob, laden with gossip of birth, death, weddings, and illnesses, as American as Anheuser-Bush and as harmless as a backyard barbecue.

The following is an interview between Lieutenant Kenneth D. Smith and Deputy Joseph Sims of the Los Angeles Sheriff's Department with Melinda Marie Custer. Lieutenant Smith and Deputy Sims have over six drawers of information about any and all outlaw motorcycle clubs that have or still do operate in the continental United States. The interview was conducted in September, 1972.

Q: What is the correct title of your division, how long has it been in existence, and what is your territory?

A: We're the Gang Unit, which includes keeping track of outlaw motorcycle gangs. Our territory is really the entire United States. They're so mobile. But we concentrate on California and work to supply other departments with information as well as the attorney-general's office.

Q: What specifically brought about the formation of such a unit—the preponderance of outlaw gangs?

A: Yes. Because of the law-enforcement problems the unit's been around for about ten years in various divisions. But now we're our own unit.

Q: Would you define, according to the guidelines of your department, the difference between a "straight" and an "outlaw" club?

A: You'd have to contact the AMA about the straights. We've no contact with them at all. The outlaws, well, to determine an outlaw you have to take into account the amount and type of crimes involved. And especially their general attitude.

Q: Antiestablishment?

A: No, not really—they're always battling with the antiwar demonstrators. It's a lawless attitude. They wear an FTW (Fuck the World) patch. The only laws they follow are their club's.

Q: Could you give me a brief history of the local outlaw groups, i.e., what gang was first on the scene, did they grow due to splits, antagonism, etc.?

A: The clubs were probably formed when the motorcycle was invented. The most famous, of course, is the Hell's Angels (HA's), which started up in the forties. It's really the number one status club nationally. They get along with another club, the Pagans, but still others like the Road Regents are not acceptable to the HA's. The majority are formed this way, they just can't make the HA standards. I think also the Galloping Goose was formed out here early in the forties, too.

Q: Which do you consider the most antisocial, abnormal, or what have you—in order of their impact on this area? Also, could you give me the names of their current leaders, where they might be contacted, plus their fraternal insignias, signs, and if they prefer certain bikes?

A: I can't give you names. *Smith gave him the nix wink at this point to clam up on names, specific locales.* They all like the Hogs (Harleys) or, more recently, the Honda 750. It's about a 75/25 ratio for the Hogs. And I can't really give you any exact location other than their home-base town. They're extremely mobile.

The top group is the HA's; have been and always will be. Recently the Hessians (south Los Angeles) and the Vagos (San Gabriel Valley) have been giving us trouble. Orange County's had the most trouble of late, four or five Hessian murders currently. The Hessians' patch (termed "colors," patched cutoff Levis jacket) is a Maltese cross with a skull on top and a sword extending through it top to bottom. The bottom patch is their territory, Hessians So. Cal.

The Vagos (Spanish name meaning tramp, wanderer, nomad, gypsy) are presently giving us the most trouble: murder, rape, oral copulation, sodomy, etc. . . .

Q: Vagos, with that name, then, would it be exclusively Mexican-American in membership?

A: No. They have about 150 members and are now very active in San Gabriel Valley area. Their patch is a horned dragon with outstretched arms and claws above a winged cycle wheel.

In my opinion, there's not a club in California that doesn't exist without the HA's approval. But you can never wear the HA's red and white colors. Like the Losers (Fresno) who won't even wear their colors without HA approval. Every club has its own Mamas, not a separate club.

Q: You mean there are, for example, no Angelettes?

A: Yeah. Most clubs' Mamas wear their guy's club patch with Property of So-and-So (male member's name) on their jacket. And you don't see too many "flying colors" (jacket worn when cruising streets) due to police stoppage, reasonable cause, and so on. Usually we'll find the numbers on the cycles filed, parts that have been stolen and equipment violations . . .

Q: Could we return to some other groups you consider active in Southern California?

A: The Devil's Henchmen are in the foothill area (Sunland, Tujunga). They have twenty-five to thirty members. We've had no trouble with them lately, but in the past they've been known to burn, pillage, and rape. The Satan's Slaves are a San Fernando Valley group. No trouble lately and they've also got about twenty-five members. You'd be surprised. The papers say "200 Angels are on their way to Bass Lake for the 4th holiday." But it's really only twenty-five HA's or so in the lead and the rest are tagalongs. Memberships aren't that big. Though we've got thirty thousand cards here on file, you've got to remember that these include associates, known friends of a group's member, and the like.

The Comancheros, a San Bernardino gang, no longer exist. I guess they went out about five years ago.

The Road Regents, well, you see a few patches here and there, but for all practical purposes they're a defunct club (previously Long Beach based).

The Coffin Cheaters came in the mid-fifties with red and white colors. The HA's colors. The HA's didn't like this and told them right off, "You'll join or we'll do ya." So, in effect, you might say they merged with the HA's. They became the Los Angeles County chapter of the Angels, but that went out of existence in January of 1970. Now, there are two different sides as to why there's no HA in L.A. County. The HA's say the membership was low so they pulled the charter. We'd tell you that so many were arrested at one incident that the national HA president didn't like it and pulled the charter.

The incident was in San Gabriel in 1970. A funeral for a dead HA. At the wake afterward, for the deceased member, things went out of hand. Twenty-seven members were actually jailed.

The Challengers are also now defunct. (This is the group, not the HA's, that gang-banged an officer's daughter; he shot one of the defendants at the trial. The defendants were convicted, the officer let off from the force, but acquitted of criminal charges.) That officer and his daughter's incident pretty much killed that in about 1967.

Q: Is there any specific age group that is attracted to these gangs? Can you give me a mean or average age?

A: HA's have to be twenty-one, minimum. One HA in the files was born in 1927 —forty-five years old and has a son who is an associate (because he's not yet twenty-one). Only no-class clubs would take anyone under twenty-one.

Q: Has there been any infighting that we used to read about so much five or six years ago?

A: Not too long ago the Hessians had been fighting with the Seekers (Orange County). Four or five murders or shootings we told you about earlier. But the Seekers have moved back to Pennsylvania. So that one's over.

Q: I'd like, for a moment, to return to the Satan's Slaves. I understand that they were somehow involved with the Manson family at the Spahn ranch prior to the Tate murders. Could you enlarge on the tie-in, the why or wherefore?

A: Yes, the Straight Satans (Venice gang) were more prevalent with Manson. But the Slaves were there too. I guess they were there for the broads and dope. Manson did have a bevy of young things. I can't really say whether they actually split before the murders or not. But I can say that Bob Beausoleil and Manson under an AKA (also known as) were probably past members or associates . . .

Q: Then you'd have to conclude that at least two bike-gang members were convicted in the Tate case. . .

A: No. You're not a member unless you're wearing the colors. Neither were, and I really feel they were just associates from the past. Membership is strict: tattoos, colors, membership cards. You know that under California law the HAs are incorporated and their patch is patented?

Q: I've noticed here in Los Angeles, at least, a recent emergence of blacks on choppers. Do they have any exclusive, militantly black clubs?

A: No, not exclusively or militantly black that is. There is the Chosen Few (south central Los Angeles). Another chapter of theirs, in Pasadena, is integrated and the San Gabriel chapter is mostly Chicanos. The mother organization in Los Angeles has existed for about twenty years. Comparatively, they don't have that many brushes with the law because at their functions they police themselves.

Q: Speaking of policing by gangs, are you familiar with the Altamont incident where it's been printed that the Hell's Angels were policing the stage at the 1969 Stones concert?

A: Well, either the Stones or their promoters or someone connected like that did sanction the HA's policing effort at Altamont.

    I don't want to libel anybody, but I really can't believe it was sanctioned by the law-enforcement agencies. I mean a dude was killed in that.

Q: Back, if I may, to the Chosen Few. Would you consider these a direct antithesis to the Iron Cross Club?

A: The Iron Cross . . . I don't even know if they have any cycles anymore. They wear those swastika things for shock value only. Some show up at American Nazi rallies and parties, but as for being active, we've not seen much. The best place to find them would probably be at Nazi-party headquarters. I don't know whether the Nazis sanction them, but they're there.

Q: We're reading/hearing less and less of the Angels and their antics, as well as other outlaw groups regarding public brawling, forced sexual perversions, etc. To what do you attribute this—law crackdown, youth turning to social change as opposed to just kicks?

A: As far as the HA's go, they don't have to build a name for themselves anymore. I don't know if it's this social involvement or not. If someone's going to be an outlaw, they will. It's just not been given much press play really. I honestly believe that active membership and recruiting is just as high as it ever was. Law enforcement knows that their law troubles are not on the downswing, but the layman doesn't because it's not publicized anymore.

Q: Would you say that the emergence of so-called straight clubs such as the Hollywood Playboys have curtailed the outlaws?

A: No. I would say no. Again, if they're going to be bad, they're bad.

Q: Do you know of any exclusively female clubs?

A: There are none. None at all.

Q: What would you say would be the mean/average cycle injury rate?

A: I have no statistics. But I'll tell you that if they crash, they do a good job of it.

Q: Have I missed any important aspect you wish to comment on, i.e., is your department aiding/encouraging straight clubs to curtail the outlaws?

A: We don't have any programs for any groups. But we certainly don't discourage the straights. We're called on a lot by private citizens because the outlaws destroy property—the terrain, watershed areas, fire areas, noise, and so forth. All we do is keep track of the outlaws to assist other divisions with information on AKAs, members, IDs, and with solving crimes.

One thing we didn't mention. The HA's Old Ladies don't wear a patched jacket with property of —— on it like the others.

Q: One last question, if they're not flying their colors, how can Mr. America, Joe Average who only reads of the HA's, recognize that he might be in trouble in an off-ramp with thirty bikers or so?

A: If there's a bunch of people on choppers, I'd say get the hell out of there. They may do nothing. They may make fun of you. A lot of trouble starts when a gang makes cracks about a man's wife and he gets out of the car to show his masculinity. Well, he comes out on the short end of the stick obviously and might be endangering his wife at the same time.

Following is a copy of the department's official listing of outlaw-biker terms:

Bible: the Harley manual

Class: doing the spectacular in their nomenclature, that is urinating in the street in front of God and the public

Crash: drunk and pass out

Brown eye: the act of pulling down pants and spreading cheeks

Flash: vomit

Garbage wagon: stock cycles

Mamma: female; new associate of club available to any and all

Old Lady: female; property of particular member only

Put: just cruising around town

Jam: on a run, i.e., the highway to Bass Lake

Snuff/Dusted: killed

The following is an interview with a twenty-seven-year-old member of the Hell's Angels Motorcycle Club. He preferred to remain nameless and was not wearing the Hell's Angels' colors at the time of the interview. The impression he gave was that of being totally stoned, very restless and generally defensive. This was not, according to him, the first time he'd been interviewed, and he mentioned several times that he should be paid for the interview, since he'd been quoted in the *Saturday Evening Post* and filmed by a CBS man whose name he didn't remember. He did not ride his chopper but drove a Ford Mustang which he said belonged to his "old lady." He glanced toward the door several times and seemed to inspect every person entering the establishment. The interview has been drastically edited, as a goodly portion of it, when replaying the cassette it was taped with, was incoherent.

Q: How long have you been an Angel? And what did you do before that?

A: I rode with 'em for a year before I got my wings, and I've been with 'em for about six years now and I live with two brothers. Before that, I was in the Army, then I was a mechanic for a place in Berdoo, and a cook.

Q: Were you always into bikes, or did that come after you got interested in the Angels? Why did you join them anyway?

A: Yeah, I was always into bikes, man, always. I had this incredible piece of shit, an old Indian, like when I was about fifteen, and I farted around with some Japanese garbage machines for awhile, did some flat-tracking. Then I got into Harleys, which is how I met the Angels in the first place, though I'd heard of 'em of course, like everybody's heard of the Angels, and I chopped the hog and spent this fucking bundle of bread on it. Then I started riding with 'em, the Angels I mean, I really dug it, you know, like I'd found my place. Listen, I'd been canned from everything, and I was a cook, a fuckin' cook, in the Army. Said I was too small for the infantry or some sort of bullshit, and I ended up cooking for all these assholes. So when I split, it was just normal that I'd end up with those dudes. Hell, they're all as fucked up as I am 'cause listen, man, I know I'm fucked up. That's why we're strong, man, 'cause we all know we're fucked up . . .

Q: Are the Angels as tough as they're said to be? Or is that mostly legend.

A: Tough? Shit man, you couldn't put us down with fuckin' sledge hammers! Yeah, but like everybody says we cause trouble, and that's bullshit, 'cause what happens is that some local asshole decides he's gonna try himself against us and he gets stomped, 'cause like we don't fuck around at all, and when somebody gets up against us, we don't play footsy with the dude, right? But we don't start stuff, we don't start trouble. Shit, trouble comes to us, man. And like we always get accused of crap like rapes and we don't rape people, you can't call it rape when the chick lies back and wants it?

Q: If the Angels are so tough, how come it took me three days to find you, and you don't want me to use your name?

A: Man, you're some kind of asshole too, aren't you? Right now, right this minute, half the cops of San Francisco, Oakland, and L.A. are looking to waste Angels. Try riding a chop in L.A. They'll pick you up and hassle the shit out of you, and then they'll throw away the key. We ain't exactly the most popular people around, you know. So what we're doing now while Sonny (Sonny Barger, president of the club) does time is lay low. 'Cause if we show ourselves, you're gonna get wiped out. We ain't dead, though, we're just kinda sleeping . . .

Q: Is it true you've got homosexuals in the club?

A: Man if we found out one of the brothers was a fag he'd get his balls kicked to jelly. There's always some queers hanging around who want to give head to the whole club, but they look for us, we don't look for them. Shit, we've got some of the most beautiful broads in California dying to get balled and you think we're gonna turn fag? Listen, we've got about fifteen broads who can take on the whole club and then beg for more. We don't need fags. People say we're fags 'cause they just don't understand how tight we are with each other. Like the club's gonna be your mother and father and son, man.

Q: Were you at Altamont?

A: No man, I was in the hospital during Altamont. I don't know anything about Altamont.

Q: Do you think the guy pulled a gun?

A: If Sonny said the nigger pulled a gun, he pulled a gun. I told you, I don't know anything about Altamont.

Q: What about the charges that Angels are smuggling dope in from Mexico?

A: I don't know anything about that either. The only time I went to Mexico was to get laid.

Q: How long are you going to remain with the Angels?

A: Probably till I die, man. Those crazy fuckers are probably gonna kill me yet. (Laugh) Shit. Where the fuck do you want me to go, man? Get another job? Get canned, and then what. No, these are like my brothers, man. That's why we kiss each other and do other weird shit. We're all the same blood . . .

3

"Charley's Life
or What to Do When You Got It"

The machine is sitting in the driveway and everyone in the neighborhood thinks old Charley has finally flipped, gone off the deep end, spending the price of his wife's expected mink coat on this contraption, which is, it must be admitted, really something to look at, what with all the chrome and wires and cables hanging left and right. But then, old Charley's always been something of an eccentric. Charley's first motorcycle is one of those big Limey twins that have thunder in their guts and leave oil puddles on the clean suburban driveway, which was originally conceived to harbor a station wagon, not a motorcycle.

Old Charley comes out, alone, and everyone just knows that his wife is weeping heavy tears in the bedroom, tears which manifest the vanishing of the mink coat and the discovery of a brand-new Charley, one she never even suspected existed. Charley's wearing a brown-leather jacket (the motorcycle caused enough of a stir, and a black-leather jacket would probably get him sent off to the asylum by a bunch of well-meaning friends), blue jeans tucked into motocross boots, gloves, and a full-coverage helmet. He looks kind of funny. Charley nods at people, sensing his moment of glory, his chosen time to make believers of all those heretics. Charley has memorized the owner's manual, almost, so he walks around the machine looking very professional, tugging here and there at a cable and hitting the brake and clutch levers, pushing the rear end down with a heavy hand for the pleasure of watching it spring up again. Beautiful day. Wishes of a life-time finally granted, because Charley has wanted a motorcycle for years and years and has never had the opportunity to get one, with the rising costs of everything and the mortgage and college educations for three kids. This is the fruition of a dream, Charley's own mountain top finally conquered.

The neighbors are out, and though some look quizzical, others are damned envious. Charley mounts his beast, pulls the choke lever the way the dealer told him to, and kicks once, hard. The machine kicks back once, hard, and Charley muffles an expression of intense pain. He smiles. He kicks again, and again, and again, and the cycle doesn't oblige him with so much as a sputter. The looks of awe are tainted with faint smiles now, and Charley's getting red. The helmet's getting damned hot, and there's a slight film of sweat around his brow. He's biting his lower lip, which luckily no one can see. He kicks again and suddenly remembers that a bike is not like a car. He forgot to turn the gas on. A few people turn around and plan to leave, obviously getting bored with the eccentric's attacks on his machine. Charley hurriedly turns the gas on, fearful of losing his audience, tickles the carbs and kicks down hard. The bike lights up with a roar that would deafen an elephant and whoever was going to leave isn't going to leave now. Charley straddles it, pulls in the clutch, and pops it into first, revving the machine repeatedly to keep the engine warm lest he must start the whole rigmarole again. He eases the clutch out and the machine shudders a little, moves forward and lunges. Charley panics and pulls in the clutch, lets it out again with no gas on and staggers down the street. He makes a wide U turn, feet off the pegs, and the machine is still bucking. Charley turns it on, dropping the clutch and hitting the throttle and the machine roars, belches, spits, stands up on its rear wheel, a motorized stallion no less, with Charley hanging on for dear life and reacting instinctively, curling his wrists and pulling back, his right foot waving in the air and finally alighting on the rear brake, which seems to stop the machine in midair, an even more frightening experience, so he chooses the lesser of two evils and hits the throttle again and the Limey twin is bounding like a Texas jack rabbit in heat, up on the sidewalk and off the sidewalk into Mrs. Troy's rosebushes, all the way on the rear wheel with Charley hanging on like a starving leech. The neighbors have scattered and Charley's wife is standing on the doorsteps with a wide O for a mouth, holding her hands up to her cheeks. She closes her eyes as Charley smashes into Mrs. Troy's garage. The machine, throttle stuck open, lies on its side, roaring and shaking like a beached whale. There's a tinkle of broken glass as the headlight lens collapses into various asymmetrical pieces, and in the slim instant before losing consciousness, Charley thinks that, after all, his earlier resolve to learn to ride in the parking lot at midnight might have been followed with better results.

The moral of the story is never to show off until you've mastered the machine, or, better, never show off, period, because motorcycles are oftentimes quirky things with mean temperaments and tricks stashed away to surprise even the experts.

The instructions given by dealers upon delivery of a bike to customers are at best cursory ones. This lever does that, and this one does that, and the pedal brakes the whole thing if you're going too fast. Unfortunately, it just isn't so simple, which is why the great majority of cyclists killed on the roads are inexperienced ones, on their first and last machines.

All motorcycles are basically the same, with the exception of small "automatic" models, which need no clutch. The others have four main controls. By 1973, these controls were standardized according to an order issued by the Department of Motor Vehicles. The rear brake is activated by pressure on the right pedal, the transmission is operated by the left pedal. Throttles are always on the right, as is the front brake lever. The clutch lever is on the left. Anyone capable of driving a car can ride a motorcycle. Coordination is necessary, true, but again in no unusual amount.

The basic things one must remember when driving a motorcycle are actually few. A bike is generally far more powerful and responsive than an automobile, but, at the same time, is lighter and smaller, harder to see and easier to dump. At speeds, it's as stable as a car and tracks far better if well-equipped and well-ridden. It must be driven defensively, for the streets abound with nuts, careless drivers, seemingly blind people, and individuals whose reflexes are better geared to walking than driving. Motorcycles make motorists angry, for reasons unknown, and a biker should keep in mind that many, many people still consider motorcycles the kind of vehicles to be relegated to the sidewalk.

The break-in period of a bike is by far the most important running time it will have. A poor rider can, in half an hour, destroy a machine or, worse, lay himself down to years of trouble. A new machine with no mileage is delivered with a tight engine. The rings, valves, clutch, gear train, and brakes are tightly matched and prone to overheating, which could and does score the cylinders, warp, bend, and total an engine with amazing ease. All machines should be broken in carefully, and though times and distances do vary, it's wise to ride softly for at least the first eight hundred to one thousand miles. As a rule, the first three hundred miles should be ridden below half the red line on the tach; from three hundred to six hundred miles occasionally blip the engine without red-lining it. From six hundred to one thousand, ride at your leisure, shifting speed and rpm, but don't try to get to the top speed. Change the oil once every three hundred miles, and calculate a ten-minute cooling period for every hour ridden. The brakes should be applied with care the first few miles, to insure proper seating of the brake shoes or, in case of disc brakes, the brake pads.

Each motorcycle, of course, requires attention to its peculiarities. A chopper will not be ridden like a Dunstall Norton, which will not be ridden like a Honda 350. A road rider hitting the dirt in street fashion will mangle himself painfully. Styles differ, as do motorcycle characteristics, but, on the whole, there are several things that a rider might remember to help him in times of emergency. A motorcycle is ridden in a state of equilibrium, as opposed to the four wheel stability of a car, and will therefore be highly susceptible to quick and unexpected changes of direction, i.e., getting smashed broadside by a Chevrolet Impala. What, as a rule, is dangerous to a car is deadly to a cycle. But these situations can be minimized with knowledge and practice.

A new biker whose only experience consists of a few trips down the street and up the driveway is likely fodder for the mortuary. His reflex actions will not be adjusted to high-speed traffic on a superhighway, and he'll react dangerously and thoughtlessly to events that could be avoided. Riding high speeds is an experience admittedly not for the squeamish. It is scary, windy, occasionally downright dangerous. There are constant hassles, and a rider is likely to feel somewhat akin to a gladiator trying to make it out of the circus alive. Motorists are irremediable road hogs, awash in the glory of their ambulatory coffins. Practice on the highway is essential if one wishes to really master a machine. The first thing to remember is one often overlooked: can the bike actually keep up with the high-speed traffic of a freeway, and, more important, does it have the reserve speed necessary to get the rider out of a bind? Top speeds are vastly overstated by most manufacturers, and speedometers are not to be trusted. The majority of motorcycles sold here have incredibly optimistic speedos. Machines topping out at a go-for-bust one hundred miles per hour will register, on the dial, 120. As a rule, subtract twenty to thirty miles an hour from the face of your instrument. This will give you a fairly accurate top speed. Lying down on the tank will offer another five miles an hour, but shouldn't be depended on. Accelerations gained from such acrobatics are slow ones at best, and unreliable. Lightweight machines will, of course, be far more dangerous at high speeds than heavyweights. Their lack of acceleration and, more important, the basic fact that they were not designed to be used for lengthy top-speed runs makes them accident prone.

There have been a large number of books written suggesting different riding techniques, books that can teach how to wheelie, scramble, hill climb, tour, or race. Some are excellent, others are not, but all offer a few suggestions that a new rider might be wise to follow.

The most important and elementary one is, simply, keep your cool. Chances are most riders, at least once and probably several times, encounter situations in which instinct and knowledge are contradictory. The first and most common to new riders is encountered in the turns. A motorcycle will lean, naturally, and the biker's first thought will be to lean the other way, which will make him go straight. Pillion passengers are even more prone to do this, and should be told not to panic during a long, forty-five-degree sweeper. The entire business of guiding a motorcycle is not done so much by handlebar control as by weight shifting. Once the weight is properly applied, let the machine carry you. Accelerate once you can see the end of the curve, and brake, during the curve, only with the rear wheel's brake. All very simple. Should you get into a skid or break traction for any one of various reasons (sand, water, oil, mud, etc.), don't try a panic stop. Flat trackers, the people who make skidding around on two wheels a habit and a way of life all recommend the same thing—control. Smash on your brakes and you're a dead man, or at least an injured one. Rather, let one foot run along the ground to stabilize you while straightening the rear wheel out by judicious use of the throttle. A motorcycle's natural tendency is to go straight, and the machine will stabilize itself, except in the worst of times. Should such a time come for you, bail out, after due consideration. Your body is worth much, much more than your machine.

There are, of course, the regular hazards of the road. These can be lessened by common sense. Tailgating an automobile is a foolish pastime, which can result only in back-end collision. Speeding between cars is equally dangerous. Treat and drive your bike as if it were a $25,000 Lamborghini that you have no intention of trashing after a month. It's a good idea to stay clear of the very center of the road's lane, as this area is the dumping ground for countless gallons of oil and transmission fluid. This stuff is slippery, particularly during and after the first hour of a downpour. Ride either to the left or right of the slick. The author remembers not heeding his own advice and laying the machine down near a New Jersey turnpike tollbooth, which was all very embarrassing and cost the price of a new lever and handlebars. It also strewed his camping gear around a ten-foot diameter, and a perfectly good Boy Scout mess kit was totaled when a large truck ran over it.

Watch out for water puddles, as machines have a tendency to "aquaplane" when they hit a film of water at high speeds. Aquaplaning means, quite simply, that the wheels are no longer in contact with the road and are skimming over the asphalt upon the water. Again, slamming on the brakes can be cataclysmic. Ride through it, letting the machine find its own way.

There are no set rules to follow to avoid accidents. It's all in being capable of anticipating various situations and either avoiding them or coming prepared to handle them. Bugs. Rocks. Rain. Dust. All can be dismissed if you wear the proper clothing and headgear. A good helmet with a face shield will diminish flying threats, boots and a sturdy jacket will protect both the legs and upper body in case of collision or fall. Gloves are a question of personal preference. Some wear them, some don't. They keep your hands clean, and are helpful on muggy days when sweaty palms abound, but they also diminish the tactile senses.

Winter riding is another bag altogether. Many bikers solve the problem by simply storing their machine over the winter months, thereby avoiding the discomforts of freezing temperatures. They're missing a lot, for cold-weather riding is an experience onto itself, invigorating as little else can be if the rider is properly prepared for it. There are, basically, only two things that a winter rider must consider before mounting his machine, the conditions of the roads he will ride and the wind-chill index he'll be facing. Road conditions are easily discernible. Iced-over or snowy roads should be avoided. Motorcycles, under such conditions, are simply not as drivable as stabler, four-wheeled vehicles. Check the weather reports. The other, and more important thing to consider, is commonly called the "wind-chill index." Basically, studies show that the heat the body loses because of wind and temperature can be estimated by multiplying a factor for the wind (which gets bigger as the wind increases) and a factor for temperature (which gets bigger as the temperature goes down). The resulting wind-chill index is a good guide as to what clothing will be needed for protection from the cold. At twenty degrees, for example, the chill index or equivalent temperature will vary greatly according to the speed of the motorcycle. Ten miles per hour will bring temperatures down to two degrees, twenty miles per hour will bring it down to minus nine degrees, and thirty-five miles per hour will give off an arctic minus twenty degrees. Since these measurements are effective on skin tissue, the obvious is to combat the chill factor with the best wind-resistant garment available.

Leather is still the preferred motorcycle wear. Its wind resistance is good, and in case of spills, it's the next best thing after a suit of armor. Leather's rather high cost has led to the use of leather-like garments made of artificial fabrics that, for all their similarity to the real thing, are still not as protective.

Rain-riding, though not always fun, can be enjoyable if the biker has taken the time to outfit himself properly. Your School Patrol yellow slicker won't do. It'll flap in the wind, get in the way and probably leak. Most shops sell, relatively cheap, two-piece rain suits that make you look alarmingly like a weatherproof Yeti but do a passable good job of keeping you dry. For the moneyed few who can afford them, Barbour-type suits, made in England, are by far the best. They're made of waxed canvas and can be worn in all forms of inclement weather. Gloves and boots are also a good idea.

The two major things to remember when riding in the rain is that, one, the pavement will be slick for a short while and, two, visibility is atrocious. Pavement slickness can't really be fought. The recommended thing is to buy the best set of tires you can afford and slow down. Rain will wash

WIND-CHILL FACTOR

TEMPERATURE

COOLING POWER OF WIND EXPRESSED AS EQUIVALENT CHILL TEMPERATURE

WIND SPEED-MPH	40	35	30	25	20	15	10	5	0	-5	-10	-15	-20	-25	-30	-35	-40	-45	-50	-55	-60
0	40	35	30	25	20	15	10	5	0	-5	-10	-15	-20	-25	-30	-35	-40	-45	-50	-55	-60
5	35	30	25	20	15	10	5	0	-5	-10	-15	-20	-25	-30	-35	-40	-45	-50	-55	-65	-70
10	30	20	15	10	5	0	-10	-15	-20	-25	-35	-40	-45	-50	-60	-65	-70	-75	-80	-90	-95
15	25	15	10	0	-5	-10	-20	-25	-30	-40	-45	-50	-60	-65	-70	-80	-85	-90	-100	-105	-110
20	20	10	5	0	-10	-15	-25	-30	-35	-45	-50	-60	-65	-75	-80	-85	-95	-100	-110	-115	-120
25	15	10	0	-5	-15	-20	-30	-35	-45	-50	-60	-65	-75	-80	-90	-95	-105	-110	-120	-125	-135
30	10	5	0	-10	-20	-25	-30	-40	-50	-55	-65	-70	-80	-85	-95	-100	-110	-115	-125	-130	-140
35	10	5	-5	-10	-20	-30	-35	-40	-50	-60	-65	-75	-80	-90	-100	-105	-115	-120	-130	-135	-145
40*	10	0	-5	-15	-20	-30	-35	-45	-55	-60	-70	-75	-85	-95	-100	-110	-115	-125	-130	-140	-150

DANGER OF FREEZING EXPOSED FLESH FOR PROPERLY CLOTHED PERSONS

LITTLE DANGER

INCREASING DANGER
(Flesh may freeze within 1 minute)

GREAT DANGER
(Flesh may freeze within 30 seconds)

*Winds above 40 mph have little additional effect

Adapted from Arctic Aeromedical Lab Technical Report 64-28

away the road film in a short time, so decelerate, enjoy the ride, and think of all the poor fools locked in their cars. Don't practice acrobatics right now, since braking and acceleration will be vastly diminished.

Visibility can be a hassle, particularly during drizzly times. There once upon a time existed a face shield which, at speeds, spun and centrifugally got rid of vision-hampering water, but these haven't been on the market for a long time. Get a good defogging solution and put it on the inside of your faceshield. Lastly, since other motorists' visibility will also be reduced, ride with your lights on, use your turn signals, and try to wear some sort of eye-catching clothing.

4

The Racing Game

Racing. The bone-snapping acceleration and quick flash of triumph of a successful drag run, smoking all the way down the quarter mile. The painfully planned and carefully executed defiance of gravity on a trial. The feeling of digging in at the bottom of a small mountain. The ballet-like grace of a long sweeper taken at 120 in fifth gear, crouched and deaf to all things, juggling clutch, brake, and throttle, figuring curves and acceleration.

Racing motorcycles is a fine brew of mechanical knowledge, guts, tenacity, and physical stamina. Not an easy sport by any means, nor a relaxing one. A strenuous pastime that allows few moments of rest and requires constant awareness. It's very easy to dump it—a false move, a bad reflex, a missed shift.

Hill climbs, scrambles, enduros, flat tracks, desert races, road races, drags, all sports that smell of sweat and leather, mud and gasoline, sports which at first are apparent. Catastrophe is around the next curve, the next jump. The abandon with which some of the riders handle their machines is almost suicidal.

Racing, in a surprisingly short time, has recaptured the national interest.

A 492 c.c. BMW with sidecar at the Sidecar International in 1959.

The public, in order to satisfy vicarious needs, has been tuning in to CBS "Wide World of Sports," paying the entrance fee to see and hear and smell the competition in Madison Square Garden and the Houston Astrodome, and trekking to wildcat races held in farmers' fields. The blood many come to see is rarely there, though the circus atmosphere often is. Racers, as a whole, are a careful group, and racing, as a sport, is as safe as the participants make it. Most bikers will swear their allegiance to the track or dirt and hasten to make known their distrust of regular road riding. A number of racers refuse point blank to ride on the road, citing all the dangers represented by little old ladies, dogs, buses, trucks, automobiles, and fishtailing '55 Oldsmobiles. There are no stop signs, blind curves, oil slicks, or hot rods flooring their pedals to wipe you out, no hassling cops. The track is much, much safer.

Perhaps. There's little doubt that a comparison of the accident rate on the road versus that of the track will show that the road riders are the suicidal ones. The racers, for all their broad-sliding dare-deviltry, are far more safety conscious, for more than one reason. A devoted racer will have invested an incredible amount of time, money, and sweat into the building and maintenance of his machine. He is, for the most part, not so much interested in histrionics as in performance and results, and his riding position will generally reflect his standing. Few top riders are show-offs. They're all aware of the fact that they're competing and, perhaps more significant, that they're competing against their equals or superiors. The inevitable spills are rarely as lethal as they might seem, and what appears deadly rarely is, though sprains and broken bones are relatively common.

Some races, particularly those held indoors, take on an almost gladiatorial aura. The racers, resplendent in leather pants and jackets decorated with anything from four-leaf clovers to Stars and Stripes, stride into the middle of the track in an orderly line, helmet under right arm. The crowd cheers. The national anthem is played. Everybody stands. The racers file out and everybody stands and cheers. The races are announced by a bastardized form of Spanish bullfighting music while a master of ceremonies with a tense and rusty voice introduces the "boys" who come from Wilmington, Delaware, and Poolesville, Maryland. He takes special care to point out the winners of previous events, the injured of a week ago, and the courageous one "who broke off his cast, ladies and gentlemen, just so he could make it down here tonight. That's devotion, ladies and gentlemen, and let's give him a big welcome." Everybody claps.

The races start and the announcer screeches out names, numbers, and motorcycle makes. The crowd rivets its eyes to the leader and waits for the spill. If and when it comes, it's accompanied by loud sounds of excitement from the M.C. who keeps the crowd on their feet by theorizing on the extent of the injuries and announcing the arrival of the ambulance. The crowd falls silent. A moment of respect for the fallen warrior and the race resumes.

Motorcycle racing can be divided roughly into two major parts: road and off-road competition. The first encompasses all forms involving asphalt or generally hard surfaces: flat tracking, drags, road racing, and speed runs; the second, all racing done on "loose stuff": scrambles, desert races, hill climbs, etc. Ice-racing enduros and trials are in a class to themselves. The skills needed to compete and win in any of these events vary greatly yet are based on quite similar tactics: watching the opponent and using his every mistake while applying basic knowledge to the task at hand, getting to know, in the shortest possible time, the track upon which one is racing, learning its quirks, its bumps and holes, gauging its maximum safe speed, knowing when to throttle up or down.

The machines ridden in these competitions are technological wonders, highly specialized screamers and chuggers, rarely stock, worked over and tuned to grasp the last dwindling iota of horsepower or handling. They're often expensive, far more so than their stock counterparts, need large doses of loving care and understanding, and, in the end, are utterly useless for anything save the race, the seconds, hours, or minutes of thrills that culminate endless efforts.

The American Motorcycle Association has held a tight rein on American racing since its very beginning in 1924. In 1972, the AMA sponsored or endorsed more than seven thousand races of every classification. More than 3,800 professional motorcycle racers hold AMA licenses, and a large percentage of the organization's 200,000 members race in classes ranging from amateur to expert. It's virtually impossible to make any money on a track unless one is a card-carrying AMA member, since the biggest money races are held beneath AMA banners and limited to AMA members. The AMA can disqualify a racer or a machine for any one of various occasionally dubious reasons, and has been known to pull some stunts of doubtful taste, much to the dismay of racers, promoters, and spectators alike. Viewed from another angle, the almost half a century old association has pulled

Racing knows few age limits. Tom Norris, nicknamed "Li'l Tommy," races and wins. In 1971, he was ranked in the top ten for his district in Maryland. He's fourteen years old.

Indoor racing is being rediscovered. Popular during the earlier years of motorcycling, the sport fell, vanished, and is now making a resurgence. Madison Square Garden, the Houston Astrodome, and the Baltimore Civic Center have all hosted indoor races, both for amateurs and professionals.

It's not all winning and glory. Situations such as this one are common. Spills abound, though serious injuries are rare.

bike racing from a greasy pastime to a leading spectator sport, replete with television and media coverage.

In revolt against the AMA are thousands of racers who prefer not to be members and sponsor their own activities, wildcat races, and rallies. These are held on abandoned airstrips, private property rented for the day, or deserted countryside and feature prizes occasionally collected by passing the hat around. The AMA disavows these forms of competition and ranks them roughly with the "outlaw" one percent activities.

The twenties and thirties saw dirt and board-track racing. Incredible leather-bonneted men hunched over wide handlebars thrilled the crowds as they whipped their machines to sixty and seventy mile-per-hour speeds. The late sixties and early seventies are the road-racers' years. The question, then, is how to get into racing as a privateer without bankrupting the family. The machines now being raced and sponsored by manufacturers are far too costly and far too rare to fall into private hands. They're cherished jewels upon which individual companies have lavished untold wealth and efforts, and the racers chosen to ride them are pros in the full sense of the word: factory people whose sole object in life is to beat other factory people. It helps the advertising. The day of the privateer who, alone or perhaps sponsored by a backyard shop and a welder, trounced his better-heeled opponents is virtually gone. The technical knowledge needed to build a 110 horsepower seven-speed machine is perhaps not lacking, but the facilities to do it are. Which leaves the potential racer with a number of choices, the first being simply what he wants to get into and the second how much he wants to spend getting into it.

Road Racing

Road racing is all in all perhaps the easiest and cheapest way to get into the sport. All you need is a bike (the same one you ride every day), a few dollars' worth of licensing fees, and a certain amount of guts. That and a nearby track that sanctions production bike racing will get you started.

A production machine is exactly what its name implies: a mass-produced motorcycle available to the general public. Fifty such machines must have been sold or at least produced and made available before you can get on the track with one. In order to put a bit of spice into the proceedings, the machines may be modified somewhat. The rulebook states that carburetion

Jumps have delirious effects both on crowds and jumpers. Most scramble courses have at least one or two hairy ones that occasionally catch the rider by surprise. The rider might flip his machine, if he keeps leaning back.

Dirt tracking in 1941. Girder forks, rigid frame, and sprung seat with pillion pad.

Everybody smiles, except the man on the machine. They've been called weekend gunfighters.

and electrical equipment must remain stock as must the shape of the camshaft, bearings, and the compression ratio. You can't change the transmission, but you can play around with the rear sprocket and clutch lining and overbore the cylinders to a maximum of plus .040 inches. You can change the seat, too, as well as the position of the foot pegs. The rest of the machine must remain totally stock.

The bikes will be checked, lest some nimble-fingered tuner try to fool the people. The lights and other instruments furnished with the machine must work. All that's left is to use liberal amounts of masking tape on all the lenses, remove the side and kickstand, and decide which class you're going to compete in.

Prod-racing classes run roughly like this: Micro Lightweight, 0–50 c.c.;

Liter Lightweight, 5–100; Ultra Lightweight, 101–125; Infra Lightweights, 126–175; Lightweights, 176–250 c.c.; Junior, 251–350; Senior, 351–500 c.c.; and Open, 501–1,000. These classes include everybody except a Harley-Davidson 1,200 c.c. rider.

Lest one think it's all amateur play, it should be mentioned that quite a few pros keep and race prod-class machines on the side either for fun or practice, and that among the open-class machines, speeds pass well above the kilo mark.

Most people interested in racing prods will stick to their road bike, but quite a few companies make production racers that closely approximate Grand Prix racers. One of the better ones that avoids many a rule by being furnished with a racing fairing, disc brakes, and a multispeed gearbox is the Norton production racer. It's expensive and very, very fast, runs in the open class, and wins. Yamahas, Hondas, Kawasakis, and Suzukis dominate most other classes.

Production is promoted and sponsored by two national organizations who will send information on request. The American Federation of Motorcyclists (AFM) and the American Cycle Association (ACA) are both quite active in the sport. The American Motorcycle Association to date does not have prod-group classes, preferring apparently to stick to Grand Prix machines.

If production racing is an up and coming form of motorcycling, sportsman racing so far is the most important form of motorcycle competition in the states. It involves relatively little money, is strictly for fun and trophies, and, according to the AMA, popular enough to warrant thousands of races in virtually every part of the country each year.

Sportsman racing is primarily dirt racing in its various forms: motocross, scrambles, hare scrambles, enduros. Getting into any of these competitions is more expensive than prod racing but still within the means of the average rider. The first step is to get an American Motorcycle Association membership form. You can't race AMA sponsored sportsman events unless you're a card-carrying AMA member. The AMA card will cost some $2 and the district sportsman card (which identifies you as a motorcycle racer) will cost up to $3. Some crowded racing districts require a card for every event you wish to compete in, so you might conceivably spend up to $20, which is still dirt-cheap. If you've got something against joining the rank and file of the AMA and live in the Western part of the country, the ACA promotes

By the late 1950's, streamlining was the name of the game. Machines were lower, faster, more agile.

many motocross races yearly on both a professional and amateur level. The National Off-Road Racing Association specializes in professional long-distance off-road stuff, but membership and entry fees are quite costly in comparison to the other two associations. In California, the California Motocross Club is quite active in off-road racing while Intersport helps further the sport on the East Coast.

The main expense incurred by a would-be racer will be the purchase of a dirt machine. The everyday drive-to-work-and-back-home motorcycle will not do, even if it's one of the erroneously named "street scramblers." Dirt

A 499 c.c. Norton with sidecar coming out of the curve. Streamlining a sidecar rig is completely different from streamlining a solo bike. Sidecars have a bad tendency to lift while going through left-hand turns, and this factor must be kept in mind when designing a fairing.

The off-road people: up and down ditches . . .

. . . wading across streams . . .

bikes are very particular animals made for little other than what the name implies. The temptation will be to purchase a cheap used machine in the hope of rebuilding it and making a superzapper. The cheap machine will probably end up costing far more than a new one, and, on top of it all, will not be competitive.

The first thing to decide, once all application blanks have been filed and duly returned, stamped and signed, is exactly what form of racing you want to compete in, and, perhaps more important, what category. Motocross is a rough and tumble closed-circuit racing that requires a tremendous amount of coordination and physical stamina. It's highly popular, highly competitive, and enjoyable but takes a certain amount of practice to even qualify. TT scrambles, or simply scrambles depending on the geographic area, is a motocross with a smoother course. Speeds are higher and tuning is therefore more vital. It's a less jarring sport than motocross but still requires healthy muscles and endurance.

Once the sport has been chosen, the rider should take into account (1) the size of his wallet, (2) the riding or racing experience he has had, and (3) the amount of guts, stamina, and health he's willing to invest. All these should go toward making the initial decision on the machine's engine size. Few road riders, even experienced ones, should initially venture into racing on large displacement machinery. Big bikes are harder to handle and demand much more from the rider than small machines do, and a new racer would best accustom himself to a small-displacement motorcycle before tackling the fire breathers. Since spills are common, particularly among new racers, and since lightweight machines don't hurt as much as heavy ones when they land on you . . .

The sportsman circuit was, and to a certain extent still is, dominated by European middle-range machinery. The Spanish Ossa, Bultaco, and Montesa are recurrent trophy winners, as is the British-made AJS.

Sach, CZ, and Maico motorcycles, all European, are also frequent winners. The past few years have seen the development of excellent Japanese dirt machinery, with the major Nipponese manufacturers creating some well-built and highly competitive bikes ranging from 90 c.c. to 500 c.c. in hopes of securing the evergrowing American market. Yamaha took the lead, soon to be followed by Suzuki and Kawasaki. Honda, for the first time, chose to hang back and, as of this writing, has not created a really superior dirt racing bike.

. . . and plowing through the mud . . .

A motocross racer, after. Not the cleanest sport in the world. Motocross requires energy, stamina, skill, and an ability to withstand flying mud, water, stones, and other racers.

The early days of motorcycle speed attempts brought out some strange home-built vehicles. In 1936, Art Senior, a motorcycle racer from Sydney, Australia, decided to streamline both himself and his machine. He did this by pounding sheet metal plates to shape and riveting them to his bike. Not satisfied with this, he streamlined his helmet. Then he went 123 miles per hour.

The sport includes quite a bit of daredevilry and contortionism. These riders are competing in the Coronation Grand Prix Motorcycle Race held in London, May 14 and 15, 1973. A. H. Horton is leading on a Norton followed by G. H. Taylor on an Ariel. The passengers, called "monkeys," are unidentified.

What it takes to be Number One. Mark Brelsford raced 1973 with the coveted 1 plate on his Harley. Proficiency at high speed road racing and . . .

. . . an equal amount of skill at flat-tracking his Harley made him the AMA's Grand National Champion for 1972.

The racing motorcycle should be chosen according to the races competed. There is enough specialization now for one to choose a machine virtually custom-made to one's needs. A dirt machine as a rule needs an excellent suspension coupled to a strong and reliable engine. The lighter motorcycle is better, but things such as comfort should not be sacrificed to gain a few ounces. Varying gear ratios and tires should be considered in view of the terrain encountered.

The final accessories the rider needs are good leathers and the best helmet and visor available. From then on, he's on his own.

The professionals, the 3,900 men who make a full-time living from competing in the national and international circuit, must, in general, master the skills involved in various different forms of racing. There aren't many people around who can do it. The sport ages its addicts rapidly, and only a few pros weather it well enough to get into middle age and still choose competition over the opening of a California motorcycle shop. But there's the money, and the thrills, and the crowds. Racing the big ones is a once-in-a-lifetime feeling that nothing else can approximate, they say. You stay up half the night doing the last little bit of fine tuning, careful to build up the very fine edge you'll need for tomorrow, yet willing to sacrifice the necessary sleep for the innate knowledge that once on the track, it's you, your machine, and God. And when the starter gun goes off, the world is gone until the last lap, which will spell either victory or defeat and nothing in between.

To both the initiated and uninitiated, two races stand out as the pinnacle of the season. One, Daytona, for being the biggest and richest, filled with racing names and super multithousand-dollar machines and the other, Bonneville, for being without a doubt the fastest and most exotic. Both races are sponsored by the American Motorcycle Association, both draw wide-ranging interest from manufacturers, promoters, and racers who realize that now it's the big times, *The Races*, the ones that will make more money and sell more motorcycles than any other event of the season.

Bonneville Motorcycle Speed Week stands alone, far too different from other forms of competition to be included in the mainstream of motorcycle racing, a class entirely by itself, complete with its addicts who show up once a year to inspect the salts, the ruts, the sun, the dust, and each other, complete with its own breeds of two-wheeled monsters built, tuned, carted for this one event, an event important enough to make both an automobile

Cal Rayborn piloted this single-engined Harley Sportster Streamliner to a new world speed record: 265.492 miles per hour, to be exact, on Utah's Bonneville Salt Flats.

and a motorcycle manufacturer name the top-of-the-line vehicle after it. Bonneville is a speedfreak's Christmas, big, not all that long, but flat, flatter than most any place on earth and custom-made for speed attempts that can't be approached on the quarter-mile asphalt, or the half-mile dirt track.

The Bonneville Salt Flats are located in Utah, lost in the wilds and far from any major city. There are between five and eight miles of salts that, during the winter months, are submerged, only to reappear in spring flat and smooth. And it's on these few miles that such incredible machines as Don Vesco's 182 mile per hour 250 c.c. streamliner run, throwing up great plumes of white salt ten feet into the air, occasionally wobbling at far too high speeds to become either airborne or sledlike and spin out of control.

Some have said that the Salts are too strange to enable a man to do his best. If you're sitting on the line waiting to start, everything looks as if it's uphill, and if your run has been good, you'll feel you're coasting. It's also eerie to race alone. Most bikers, new or experienced in some form of competition, have always raced against someone, or something. At the Flats, they're racing against an abstraction—time.

The days start early, before the sun and reflections of the Salts have time to fry whatever part of your body is not covered. You've got two

Munro getting ready for the Salts. He's been going there for thirteen years, each time with the same machine.

The final push. Munro on his Indian, complete with girder front end, making it probably the oldest machine to compete on the Salts.

miles to attain top speed, and a quarter-mile trap that will be timed. If you qualify by surpassing the existing record by 1/1000 of a mile per hour or better, you're in, at least for the next day for a two-way run when things start getting complicated. It's that next morning that you'll make the obvious mistake and barrel down the straightaway, watching records crumble and pushing your rpms to their limit and forgetting that regardless of the speeds attained on the way up, you've still got to make it back.

If you make it back and get a record, your only satisfaction will be to see your name in a small record book. No crowd adulation, no trophy or kisses from the trophy girl.

Bonneville Motorcycle Speek Week is, basically, an amateur event sponsored by the American Motorcycle Association, but the words "amateur event" are at best misleading. The people who annually trek to the Salts are amateurs in name only. Bert Munro, at seventy-two years of age, is still coming up from New Zealand with his Indian streamliner. It changes every time he brings it, and there are stories of old Bert casting his pistons in holes dug in the New Zealand dirt. In 1972, after a short hassle with the refs, over his age and the lack of firewalls, extinguishers, and other safety precautions, he did 160 through the traps.

Daytona, Florida. For one insane week every year, bikers and teams from the world over come to battle, chopper freaks come to see and be admired, accusations and insults are hurled, dismissals are fast and often arbitrary. The amateur has little chance of winning anything at Daytona and though, once in a while, a young man from a Midwest state hitherto unknown will zap everybody and carry off the trophies, the glory more often than not goes to company manufactured machines aboard which super riders roar or whine their way to victory.

The Baja 500 and Mexican 1000 are held respectively in June and November where riders pit their kidneys and machines against endless miles of rock, sand, gullies, and rutted roads. The machines run at Baja are strictly desert-bred beasties, and the race has one unique aspect: cars can run too. Its main advantage is that anyone with a machine can ride, the rankest amateur versus the most polished professional, the backyard tinkerer versus the helicopter-assisted Honda team. It gets awfully hot during the race, and riders are forced to bring enough water to last from checkpoint to checkpoint. Temperatures of 115 degrees are run of the mill, and a racer who breaks down can be in real danger. The machines ridden in the Baja

BONNEVILLE RESULTS—1973

CLASS	RECORD	DATE	NAME OF RIDER	MODEL MOTORCYCLE
A-C-50	70.666	8-25-72	Darrel Packard, Loma Linda, Calif.	Suzuki 50 c.c.
PS-A-100	87.773	8-24-72	Thomas Conway, Oroville, Calif.	Kawasaki 100 c.c.
C-AG-125	78.904	8-25-72	Jonas Minton, Sacramento, Calif.	Harley 125 c.c.
A-C-125	87.363	8-26-72	Alfred Vanacore, Hollywood, Calif.	Sachs 125 c.c.
A-A-125	103.659	8-24-72	Dale Ebersole, Denver, Colorado	Yamaha 125 c.c.
PS-AG-125	87.655	8-25-72	Robert Seim, Los Osos, Calif.	Suzuki 125 c.c.
APS-C-125	90.821	8-25-72	Alfred Vanacore, Hollywood, Calif.	Sachs 125 c.c.
APS-AG-125	111.573	8-25-72	Robert Barker, Valcourt, Quebec, Canada	Bombardier 125 c.c.
APS-A-125	110.736	8-26-72	Robert Barker, Valcourt, Quebec, Canada	Bombardier 125 c.c.
PS A-200	100.539	8-21-72	Dennis Roberston, Burley, Idaho	Yamaha 195 c.c.
C-AG-250	87.792	8-25-72	James Bail, Oak Lawn, Illinois	Kawasaki 250 c.c.
A-AG-250	110.064	8-24-72	George Root, Jr., Memphis, Tenn.	Suzuki 250 c.c
PS-C-250	138.410	8-25-72	William Vickery, Denver, Colorado	Yamaha 250 cc.
S-AG-250	172.455	8-24-72	Don Vesco, El Cajon, Calif.	Yamaha 250 cc.
C-AG-350	109.154	8-21-72	Joy Houston, Gardnerville, Nevada	Yamaha 350 c.c.
APS-A-350	129.109	8-25-72	Jack Murphy, Azusa, Calif.	Kawasaki 350 c.c.
C-A-500	131.995	8-22-72	Bob Braverman, Van Nuys, Calif.	Kawasaki 500 c.c.
A-AG-500	134.982	8-24-72	Jack Linn, Van Nuys, Calif.	Suzuki 500 c.c.
A-C-600	90.443	8-24-72	Richard Galloway, Alexandria, Virginia	Maico 501 c.c.
A-AG-600	93.963	8-25-72	Wayne Harvey, South Gate, Calif.	Kawasaki 533 c.c.
C-AG-700	112.062	8-24-72	Kris Stadelham, Manhattan Beach, Calif.	Norton 681 c.c.
A-A-700	137.603	8-25-72	Roosevelt Lackey, Jr., Mt. Clemens, Mich.	Triumph 680 c.c.
PS-AG-700	111.193	8-21-72	Jerry Berger, Reseda, Calif.	Norton 681 c.c.
APS-C-700	106.322	8-26-72	John Williams, La Mirada, Calif.	Royal Enfield 696 c.c.
APS-A-700	131.233	8-26-72	Roosevelt Lackey, Jr., Mt. Clemens, Mich.	Triumph 680 c.c.
C-A-750	160.285	8-25-71	Don Sliger, South Gate, Calif.	Royal Enfield 750 c.c.
S-C-750	133.268	8-21-72	William Giles, Tulsa, Okla.	Honda 750 c.c.
PS-AG-883	135.334	8-26-72	Dick Mankamyer, Kent, Ohio	Harley-Davidson 883 c.c.
APS-C-883	139.161	8-22-72	Don McCaw, St. Louis, Mo.	Harley-Davidson 883 c.c.
APS-AG-883	135.047	8-25-72	Storme Winter, Eureka, Calif.	Harley-Davidson 883 c.c.
A-C-1,000	128.810	8-26-72	Ron Secor, San Dimas, Calif.	Vincent 1,000 c.c.
A-AG-1,000	142.179	8-26-72	Shorts Cardwell, Dallas, Texas	Triumph 990 c.c.
PS-AG-1,000	154.673	8-22-72	Jon Minonno, Dallas, Texas	Triumph 990 c.c.
PS-A-1,000	150.756	8-26-72	Jon Minonno, Dallas, Texas	Triumph 990 c.c.
APS-C-1,000	130.367	8-25-72	Ron Secor, San Dimas, Calif.	Vincent 1,000 c.c.
APS-AG-1,000	152.757	8-24-72	Jon Minonno, Dallas, Texas	Triumph 990 c.c.
APS-A-1,000	170.468	8-26-72	Don Chaplin, Carlsbad, Calif.	JAP 500 c.c. Twin Engine
APS-AB-1,000	158.371	8-26-72	Shorts Cardwell, Dallas, Texas	Triumph 990 c.c.
APS-AG-1,200	160.705	8-26-72	Carl Morrow, Whittier, Calif.	Harley-Davidson 1,199 c.c.
APS-A-1,200	166.861	8-24-72	Roger Swim, Phoenix, Arizona	Harley-Davidson 1,200 c.c.
A-AG-3,000	173.808	8-22-72	Thomas Elrod, Saugerties, New York	Harley-Davidson 1,460 c.c. Twin engine
APS-AG-3,000	190.991	8-26-72	Thomas Elrod, Saugerties, New York	Harley-Davidson 1,460 c.c. Twin engine
APS-A-3,000	206.544	8-26-72	Warner Riley, Skokie, Illinois	Harley-Davidson 1,510 c.c.
S-AB-3,000	232.717	8-21-72	Jon McKibben, Los Angeles, Calif.	Honda 736 c.c. Twin engine

LEGEND

Frame or running gear.

    S — unlimited in design, streamlined.

    A — unlimited in design, and no streamlining.

    APS — unlimited in design, and partial streamlining.

    C — meeting equipment standards of approved motorcycles.

    PS — meeting equipment standards of approved motorcycles and partial streamlining.

Engines.

    C — meeting equipment standards of approved motorcycles.

    A — unlimited in design, but made by a motorcycle manufacturer. No restrictions on fuel.

    AB — Same as A, but limited to supercharged fuel or gas.

    AG — Same as A but limited to modified engine gasoline. Frame designation is placed first followed by engine designation.

In classifying machines, frame designation is listed first, followed by engine designation.

and Mexico races lean towards Husqvarna, DKW, Pentons or similarly rigged bikes: huge air and gasoline filters, excellent suspension coupled with lightweight and superlative handling, high-engine clearance, and knobby tires. The Baja and Mexico races are perhaps the greatest test of motorcycle and rider endurance yet devised.

In the 1973 Baja race, some rather unusual things happened. The lead bike in the opening of the fifth annual desert race cleared the starting ramp, accelerated, and promptly smashed into a policeman who crossed the machine's path. Both the policeman and the rider, forty-four-year-old Larry Bornhurst, were hospitalized, but, in true race fashion, the machine was repaired on the spot and Bornhurst's sixteen-year-old son resumed the race on his father's bike, less than forty minutes later.

He didn't finish in the top thirteen, but it's the thought that counts. To give an idea of the roughness of the race, it's sufficient to say that out of forty-nine starters, twenty-two finished, including a woman's team composed of Mary McGee and Lynn Wilson.

One race to stand out in 1973 was the forty-eighth running of the International Six Day Trials. The ISDT is considered the Olympics of motorcycling, perhaps the most prestigious race around, certainly one of the top ranking as far as motorcycle advertising is concerned. For the first time in its forty-seven years, the ISDT was held in the United States.

Historically, the International Six Day Trials was conceived as a vehicle to determine the best motorcycle manufactured. Various companies were invited to display their wares and enter their production machines in competitions designed to test what were then considered the major areas of importance. The bikes would travel roughly one hundred miles with no servicing over various types of terrains including mud, sand, stream beds, rocks, and woods. The rider would have to be familiar enough with the machine to be able to do his own maintenance quickly so as not to lose points. The importance of the race lay almost entirely in its advertising value. The machines run were supposedly totally stock, and therefore similar to the ones any buyer could purchase.

Things, of course, have changed. Manufacturers have subverted the original idea of the competition by supplying riders with special machines, and the riders are far from average. They're the top professionals, as far removed from everyday riders as sandlot baseball players are from their big league idols.

The 48th ISDT was held in a tri-state area which covered sections of Vermont, Massachusetts, and New York state in an area called the Berkshire Trail. There, some twenty-five countries matched the skill of their various teams in an array of events which ranged from sound tests (to measure the sound level of the machines) to acceleration, cross-country riding, and spare-tire changing. Czechoslovakia won for the fourth consecutive year. Great Britain was second. Austria was third. West Germany and the United States rounded out the top five.

5

Close Past and Closer Future

The mid and late 1960s were confusing times for cyclists. Suddenly faced with a barrage of increasingly slick advertising praising the open road, bikers the land over also found themselves harassed, arrested, searched, detained, and occasionally roughed up by law enforcers, both in small towns and major metropolitan cities. It seemed as if big- and small-time cops had passed the word that bikers were henceforth no-nos, undesirables to be swept off the roads and kept out of town like the outlaws of yore. It was all very strange, very frightening to suddenly be treated like a criminal by people who wore guns and threatened you when all you had in mind was a three-day weekend in Lake George, New York, lazing in the sun and stuffing yourself with Arbie roast-beef sandwiches and beer. All of a sudden, motorcycles were as risky as stolen cars, and perfectly straight college students, librarians, mechanics, and supermarket clerks were being hassled and booked on violation of local laws that no one had ever heard of and, worse, no one had ever enforced before.

The years at the end of the decade were years of revolution, a cop was a pig and a long-hair was a Commie. The rhetoric flew high and bright, often based primarily on the appearance of the person at whom the invectives were aimed. And motorcycles, well, hell, they were the revolutionaries' means of getting to the revolution.

Not all motorcycles, of course. Harley-Davidson Electra Glides were respectable, if redneck, but the little Jap machines with the high whining exhaust and the funny-looking custom jobs ridden by bearded freaks with pierced ears and obscene hand gestures, those were different. Those were obviously bad news. Those must be stopped. And in the late 1960s, the annual summer and spring rites had changed, the metamorphosis from panty raids to student destructions were bannered coast to coast. It was no longer satisfactory to get drunk and have a good brawl, an experience that almost everybody could relate to. Now, you had to get stoned, drugged up on all manners of weird dope whose names were so complicated that only initials were mentioned. All disconcerting, threatening, a rising tide that had to be stopped preferably before it infected the rest of the country.

Out on the West Coast, Hell's Angels and Satan Slaves and Gypsy Jokers were looting and raping and destroying small towns, laughing in the face of authority, the newspapers and magazines said. And they rode motorcycles. College people were rebelling, burning buildings, and letting their hair grow while listening to drug-related music. They rode motorcycles, too. The government was at a loss as to what to do to keep the lid on, and in the spring and summer, these very same hippies and yippies were drifting away from the campuses, spreading their threatening philosophies and trying to convert middle America, talking to people who might not know better than to listen. . . . Youth as a whole was suddenly endangering all that was good, clear, plain, and simple. And motorcyclists, by the very act of being mostly young and riding motorcycles, were the worst of the lot. Who could forget Laconia, Bakersfield, Hollister?

A large number of summer bikers underwent bad trips, which only served to polarize the two battling factions. It was fairly infuriating, in New York State, to be busted for not wearing a helmet by a motorcycle cop who wasn't wearing a helmet, or to be told that your motorcycle was illegal because the handlebars were too low, and shuttled out of town with your last $20 pocketed by a judge who couldn't tell a cycle from a sewing machine.

The problem was compounded by simple economics. Motorcyclists, as a rule, traveled on a severely limited budget. They brought little to the communities that they visited, their main outlay being food generally bought and eaten at the cheapest stand. They rarely spent the night in motels, preferring to camp. And they were a scruffy lot. Few people can weather days aboard bikes without looking as if they recently stepped from the nearest grease pit. Dirt, automobile and truck exhaust, mud, sand, grit, and oil tend to stain even the cleanest brow and ruin the best of manicures. The standard motorcycling clothes did little to endear the bikers to the populace, as leathers, boots, and denims were never too well looked upon. . . .

Bikers were not good for business; they had a tendency to make liquor-store owners happy, but they discouraged money-spending bucolic tourists who had read scary headlines and were disturbed by the sound of raucous motorcycle tailpipes.

Most cyclists, by word of mouth, learned to avoid the more notorious areas where they were made to feel unwelcome. There was no sense hassling the cops, and being hassled. One of the earliest lessons learned was that a biker in court will always lose, regardless of the circumstances, for judges and police officials will often go to incredible lengths to avoid placing the blame anywhere but on the biker if he is involved in an accident or altercation.

Cases range from the sublime to the ridiculous. In Washington, D.C., a judge found a motorist innocent who made an illegal left turn and caused a biker to crash because the biker, in the barrister's opinion, "shouldn't have been riding in the first place and got what he deserved." In Rehoboth Beach, Delaware, a group of cyclists carefully maintaining legal speeds in the area they knew was a speed trap were stopped, arrested, booked, and fined for going three miles under the limit and "obstructing traffic" at six in the morning. In South Carolina, a lone biker was put in jail for a broken taillight lens. In Maryland, another was booked on suspicion of driving a stolen vehicle. When the registration check assured everyone that the biker was riding his own machine, the arresting officer supported his actions by saying that the cyclist didn't "look right."

Enmity ran particularly high between cyclists and motorcycle cops, whose sense of dignity seemed to have been affronted by the influx of small machinery. The cops, aboard their overladen 1,200 c.c. Harley Police Specials, had long been kings of the roads. Few sights were more frightening to automobile drivers than the solitary flashing red light and siren that accompanied the bowlegged walk of the defender of the peace. In one swift blow, the motorcycle policeman was dethroned, not even by other Harley riders with whom they could at least share a taste for the same machinery but by smoky little fast-ass two-strokes, which could run their beloved Milwaukee iron into the ground, and complicated four-strokes, which stuttered past with smirking sounds. It was really too much to take, too much to accept lying down.

The big joke was to wave at the cops, who would never wave back, or occasionally drag them out at the red light and see them futilely gnashing teeth and throttle as they receded in the rear-view mirrors.

Retributions were quick to come. In California, police hounded cyclists —particularly chopper riders—ran checks on them, and measured everything from handlebars to seat height in hopes of finding violations. Unpaid traffic tickets and citations were enough to warrant a quick trip to the precinct and a sudden disappearance of the treasured driver's license. Justice was swift and often erroneous, lumping all bikers in one bag, unable and unwilling to differentiate between outlaw and AMA.

As if icing were necessary on the already unpalatable cake, a rash of second- and third-class motorcycle movies came out, movies that made the round of small town drive-ins and depicted the bikers as defilers of churches and funeral homes, rapists and sadists all, riding strange machinery, bedecked in chains and grime, outrageous in every sense of the word.

The pulp magazines had a heyday. Motorcycle gangs made great copy, could be slandered without the least recrimination, and actually enjoyed the publicity given them. A couple of strange pictures showing leather-jacketed Honda riders was enough to make a good color spread entitled "Angels from Hell Sack Small Town" or "Lust Battle of the Motorcycle Queens." The fact that a little research would always fail to certify the existence of the gang and, quite often, even of the looted small town was not enough. The results were that many a community suddenly was deluged by outrageous motorcycle coverage, a new wave of yellow journalism that did its best to warn against the impending menace. A biker coming in the same day as a triple feature at the Bijou and the new issue of *Male Stories* was hardly a welcomed individual.

By the early 1970s, things had settled somewhat. The enforcement of certain laws was still stacked against the biker, and being stopped and checked by a scowling cop was taken with something akin to philosophical

Touring is probably still America's number-one motorcycle pastime. The Harley-Davidson FLH 1200 is an expensive favorite that addicts call the King of the Highway.

detachment. The sheer number of machines crisscrossing the land, some ridden by perfectly normal people with no other bad habits, made it difficult to crack down as hard as in preceding years. Motorcyclists, if not welcomed, became tolerated.

With an estimated six million motorcycles ridden by five million riders in the United States, cyclists can be said to comprise one of the biggest minorities in the country. Strangely, the bikers have by and large chosen to remain politically unrepresented and have shunned away from such organizations that could aid their cause. As such, it's small wonder that bikers, as a rule, are discriminated against.

Only one motorcycle company, Harley-Davidson, has a licensed lobbyist working in Washington. The license granted in 1955 states the lobbyist represents both Harley and Cushman, but chances are his main interests rest in such unlikely places as golf-cart and police-machine manufacturing.

Honda, the biggest company in the world, has no lobbyists. Neither do Yamaha, Suzuki, Kawasaki, or any of the bigger German and British manufacturers. Some clubs attempt to keep a look out on national and local legislation, but most riders are totally unaware of government actions that attempt by various means to keep the riders off the road and out of the woods.

In their haste to prevent motorcycle accidents, legislators have failed to study their cause: The fact is that the majority of accidents in which bikers were injured were caused by cars that did not see the motorcycles. The motorists, and not the riders, should be educated. However, since virtually every voting family has at least one car, and since bothering the voters might very well result in the legislators' unemployment, motorcycles were blamed and subjected to changes.

The legislation that has so far raised the greatest furor was that requiring bikers to wear helmets. The issue of constitutionality was bandied about by garage lawyers who claimed that, after all, if a rider wanted to ride without a helmet, only his head was at stake, and that no one should have the right to protect someone from himself. All this was good for midnight discussions and editorials in all the cycle-oriented magazines, but the hue and cries heard were of little avail in most states. California, strangely enough, has escaped, as of this writing, any legislation forcing riders to wear helmets, and the law has been tested and found unconstitutional in a few states. Most riders agree in private that riding without a helmet is the sheerest form of lunacy and that the issue is not so much in the safety aspect as in the requirement. It's not that they wouldn't wear one, it's simply that they don't like to be forced to, and for good reason. There are days when a helmet is the best deterrent to riding. Helmets are heavy, stuffy, and hot. They're cumbersome as hell, and likely to be ripped off if left unattended, which forces the biker to carry his like a bowling ball everywhere he goes. And what do you do about passengers? . . . Carrying a helmet around with you is a pain, no doubt, and discourages female riders with beehive hairdos. The safety aspect of helmets is double-edged. Yes, they do protect from shock, but the protection they afford is dulled by the fact that they restrict hearing and peripheral sight. They also take away one of the very best aspects of motorcycling: the wind in the face and hair bit, which is the reason most riders got into biking in the first place. Finally, they're expensive, going for anywhere from $20 to $50 apiece. . . .

A motocross racer—before. The man is safety-conscious and aware of the multiple things which could, in one short race, happen to his head. He's wearing a strong helmet with a visor, goggles, and a mouth guard to protect him from flying rocks.

As of this writing, forty-three states, Washington, D.C., and Puerto Rico require helmets, but the laws get confusing and downright silly in some places. In Nebraska and Connecticut the law exists but is not enforced. In New Mexico, the law applies to all passengers but only those operators who are under eighteen years of age while Kansas and Oklahoma say only operators under twenty-one must wear them. Utah states that a helmet must be worn on roads with speed limits higher than thirty-five miles per hour. None of the states cited above has taken into account the prime factor: accidents involve mostly new cyclists, and it is they who should be protected.

Age and speed have little to do with the reality of accidents. An experienced seventeen-year-old doing ninety miles per hour is probably less prone to have an accident than his father who just started cycling and is trying to round the curve at twenty-five miles per hour.

What legislators couldn't do—avoid accidents—by enforcing helmet laws they tried to attain by making motorcycle licenses mandatory. There are now thirty-five states that require a special operator's license for driving motorcycles. The idea, at least in the beginning, was excellent. An automobile driver's license was no guarantee that a new biker knew what he was doing. On the contrary, a new rider reacting with "automobile" instincts to a "motorcycle" situation has great chances of wiping out.

Driving tests were conceived, tests that for the most part might strain the driving ability of a two-year-old but could certainly not even come close to deciding whether a cyclist was ready for the road. In Washington, D.C., the main part of the driving exam was a jaunt through small pylons placed at intervals on a parking lot. The rider had to show his dexterity by weaving through the pylons. If the rider got there early enough and the pylons hadn't been placed yet, what the hell, he could skip that part of the test and get on to the left-hand and right-hand turns.

Some schools, with AMA and local government backing, offer motorcycle driver education, but they are few and far between. Boy Scouts in California can get motorcycle safety patches, but again, California is so far ahead of its time that it'll take a while for the rest of the country to catch up.

If some of the proposed laws are, originally, wise ones backed up by a fair amount of thought and consideration, others seem based on what can only be called stupidity. State senators and representatives have long been the guardian of things they know nothing about, and motorcycles seem to have brought out the worst in civic leaders. One suggested all motorcycles be furnished with a ten-foot-tall pole on top of which would be placed a revolving beacon light. Another suggested seatbelts, and a Floridian thought all cyclists should wear blinking lights atop their helmets so that they might more easily be seen. In Washington, D.C., any modification to the frame of a motorcycle is illegal. In Maryland, one cannot alter the tailpipes, or have two seats on a bike. The seat must be a "buddy seat." California saw fit to pass a rear-view-mirror law, but did not specify the size of the mirrors. Some cyclists rode around with teeny little dentist's mirrors taped to their handlebars. Virginia, which passed a helmet law in 1971, did not say exactly what kind of helmet was necessary and, for a while, anything went, from firemen's helmets to World War I headgear. . . . Colorado states simply that no modifications can be made on a cycle. The state with the most laws is now New York, which requires a special driver's license, a safety helmet, eye protection, a passenger seat, passenger foot pegs, rear-view mirrors, a safety inspection at time of registration, and subsequent inspections at regular intervals. New York also requires that a biker's lights be turned on both day and night. In Nevada, the most liberal state, helmets be damned as long as you've got a motorcycle license. That's all.

An interesting battle is going on, as of this writing, in New Jersey, where highway authorities have tried to maintain the Garden State Parkway off-limits to motorcycles. The original law was a sage one, since the Garden State was a high-speed road at a time when the great majority of motorcycles were far slower than they are now and unable to keep up with traffic. The increased horsepower of the machines now being built has negated the law's only basis for existence. Ben Harroll, formerly of the International Four-Owner's Association (an association comprised of owners of four-cylinder motorcycles), purposely tested the validity of the law by having himself arrested for driving on the Garden State. Chances are the regulation will be repealed.

Another facet of legislation which is directly influencing the dirt riders is the increasing incidence of closures of public land to various forms of motor vehicles. The conservationists, perhaps wisely, perhaps not, state that motorcycles are highly injurious to nature. They tear up the top soil, disturb animals, etc. . . . They make noise, too, which when you come right down to it is probably the crux of the matter. Eight years ago, any vacant

The motorcycle, in some instances, has replaced the horse. This rider is herding bisons out in the West, and found his bike to be more tractable and cheaper to operate than any other mode of transportation.

lot, any desert stretch, or beach was good riding ground. Motorcycles were not yet numerous enough to garner too many complaints, and most riders tried to avoid populated places.

The crunch is on, though, and with more than three million dirt machines set loose in the United States, land is becoming scarcer. Dirt machines, as originally created, were little more than street machines with raised exhausts to clear obstacles, studded tires to increase traction in mud and sand, and various engine modifications to change the basic transference of power from one applied to top speed to one giving what can be referred to as "pulling" power. Larger rear sprockets gave quick acceleration as opposed to high speeds, and since the early machines were to be used basically in areas with little if any population, mufflers were sacrificed, both for weight and the added power afforded by unrestricted exhaust flow. The resulting machines were highly tractable and supremely uncomfortable cycles with stump-pulling power and sounds that could deafen unsuspecting eardrums. As the sport caught on and became more popular, the machines became more sophisticated but still relied on the open exhaust system to insure the extra horse needed.

Two-strokes laced with header pipes making a teeth-gnashing high-pitched whine and four-strokes with gargantuan belches could be found in most deserts and trailing areas, ridden by bikers who much preferred the freedom of the open land to that of the open road. Manufacturers strained to tune down the exhaust notes of the street machines in production, while dirt machines continued to be delivered with no sound restriction under the guise of "more power." Certainly, the raucous sound was appreciated by more than a few riders. Power, after all, should be heard as much as felt (a point of view shared with most people who enjoy a form of motorized competition), and a silent dirt-trail machine would probably not sell. The motorcycle sound is a cherished aspect of the sport, and any cyclist's description of his machine will be spiced by a vocal rendition of the bike's decibel output. It's very important to know whether the thing goes "vroooom" or "nyahhhhh," and many, many new bikers have gauged their first purchase not by the power or obvious advantages but by the sound. The whine of a two-stroke is that engine's main detriment. Old-timers speak with reverence of the hallowed thrum of a big single while numerous studios put out records entitled *The Sound of——Race* with jackets screaming "Hear the Yamasaki 12-cylinder pass the Gilenni 6 . . . Thrill to the roar of the start . . . Listen to the wailing of . . ." But one man's music is another's cacophony, and what the dirt boys relished did not endear them to the local populace out for a day's picnic in the woods. It was rather disconcerting to be biting on a roast beef on rye and suddenly hear the entire forest echo to the sound of a zillion buzz saws.

Motorcycle tire tracks, say conservationists, stay years and years and years, and are more dangerous to nature than a million sand, rain, or hailstorms. A lone biker can destroy a sand dune, thereby bringing on erosion. A thousand motorcycles will ruin a desert.

The logic of some of these arguments is as yet largely unproven. It is quite certain that motorcyclists do scare animals, but they at least don't kill them, which hunters do. Bikers have been accused of atrocious fox hunts in which the winner gets to crush the winded animal. Highly unlikely, but, even so, is it more atrocious than a bunch of equestrians dressed in red coats giving the fox to the dogs?

The machines were actually more of a bother than an actual danger, an irritation rather than a menace to the wildlife, and people who could all week listen to the sound of garbage disposals chewing bones, bulldozers destroying earth, and garbage cans merrily dropped from speeding sanitation trucks suddenly took it upon themselves to rid the earth of this new noise. Laws, many, many laws, were passed. Removing the baffles from a muffler became illegal. This, though enacted to stem sound pollution, was actually a boon to motorcyclists who no longer could blow out perfectly good engines by removing an essential piece of the machine's engineering. As the laws increased, the industry rose (slowly, oh, so slowly) to the challenge. Silencers were added to the end of the tailpipes, silencers, which, everybody swore, would cut the power by half. It didn't, but it did a good job of cutting the noise.

The AMA decided that races held under the AMA banners would be quiet ones, at least as quiet as possible, and totally unmuffled machines were not allowed to enter the competition. The Motorcycle Industry Council launched a "Less Sound More Ground" campaign, which caught on quite well, as motorcycle magazines redoubled their editorials in favor of silence. Clubs, both local and national, crusaded, stopping loud bikers and asking them to tone down a bit "for the good of motorcycling." The police sirens also knuckled down on loud machines, after the establishment of decibel limits was imposed in every state. The limits varied, but all stressed a return to silence.

And yet, in a way, it was already too late. Land taken is rarely given back, no matter how hard one tries or apologizes. What the conservationists and Bureau of the Interior had gained after long and arduous battle, they weren't about to yield. Public parks that had been closed, stayed closed, and posted land stayed posted.

It wasn't all the bikers' fault. The popularity of dirt riding came to an all-time high precisely when the ecological movement came to a head, and the battle lines seemed to be drawn in spite of all the good faith manifested by both parties. Bikers, once more, were put into an "everything is all the same" bag, which saw them grouped with such unlikely mates as snow-mobilers and dune-buggy drivers, all noisy, all destructive, all bothersome.

Strangely, the major manufacturers of dirt and competition machines did not try to halt the closure of lands. Sales kept climbing, though no one knew where the machines were being ridden. Honda did place some ads in major magazines like *Life*, but the ads were aimed at family togetherness, cemented by Hondas for the whole family. The other companies stayed quiet, not fully realizing that the land disappearance would eventually show up in their ledgers, with sales falling when disgusted riders would give up the dirt after searching and not finding any. Virtually every major company was a member of the Motorcycle Industry Council, but their participation did not include manpower donations to combat their creation's bad reputations.

Again, California took the lead with the creation of such riding grounds

The Kawasaki F-7 175 is a good example of a machine marketed for on and offroad use. Note high fenders, bash plate, and semi-knobby tires.

as Saddleback Park near Los Angeles, an area devoted solely to off-road vehicles, where power, noise, and other fancies could be fulfilled without the perpetual fear of the bust, all for $2 a day. There are hills, streams, tracks, trails in Saddleback, and everything to make a cyclist happy, from the greenest beginner to the toughest pro, and it's safe, far safer than any desert or sandlot or gravel pit.

This system, laying aside land for the express use of off-road freaks, is probably the trend of the future. To believe and hope that the off-road movement is simply a passing fad is as blind as it is silly. When men, women, and children have sunk their hard-earned wages and allowances into a dirt machine, it's highly unlikely that even strict legislation will keep them from enjoying both their investments and their hobbies. Had the legislation been enacted a few years sooner, it might have come off, but it's now much too late. The various motorcycle industries have now invested large amounts of money into research development, exports, and dealerships around the country. And Americans, as a breed, are not as pliable as other nationalities when it comes to heeding laws that they find too restrictive.

Several states have passed various regulations prohibiting the riding or driving of motor vehicles off the beaten path. In more than a few states, wise authorities do not attempt to enforce the letter of the law. It's much safer and far more comfortable to have all the riders in one place rather than trying to keep an eye on a disseminated few. Like keeping the pyromaniac in the fire station—at least, you know where he is. As such, virtually every county, every area, and every town that sells motorcycles has at least one if not more "secret places" where bikers and others thrash their machines in relatively wild abandon, heedless of any threat save that of an occasional police raid when the noise gets too loud for the good citizens.

The discrimination against motorcycles and motorcyclists is at best nonsensical. In this day and age of overcrowding, it's absurd to discriminate against a force that could easily solve at least part of the problem created by technology. If the trend toward conservationism continues—and there's no reason why people should suddenly decide they don't want cleaner air, water, etc.—the motorcycle shall become not an outcast or merely a pleasure vehicle but a highly useful and necessary mode of transportation.

If one is willing to look at it strictly from the point of view of available space for motor vehicles, the argument's validity becomes apparent. An automobile like the Fiat 600 or 850, the now illegal Austin Mini Cooper, the Subaru, or Honda, takes up an approximate fifty-five square feet of road space per car. Their use in densely populated areas has proved to be highly successful, when parking and paved areas diminish either from overuse or crowding. A compact sedan, such as the Vega, Pinto, Volkswagen, Toyota, Gremlin, etc., takes up some eighty square feet. A small station wagon or family sedan of moderate size (most automobiles like the Ford, Chevrolet, American Motors will fit this category) will take slightly over a hundred square feet while the utterly useless monolithic creations from Detroit (Cadillac, Olds, Imperial, etc.) take up more than 105 square feet.

A large motorcycle, with a maximum length of seven feet and a handlebar spread of three feet will take up twenty-one square feet, less than one-half that of the smallest cars now available to the public. The actual space available if only motorcycles were driven would for good purposes be a minimum of three times but more likely up to five or six times as large. Since it's unlikely that the population of the United States will grow six times in a few years, gasoline, licensing, and road taxes could be diminished or, if not, applied to better things than maintaining lounging space for mechanical monstrosities. If the multiplication of motorcycles seems unlikely, the increase of road and gasoline taxes are already here. As more roads are built to accommodate cars whose sizes always seem to grow, so more money will be needed to maintain the roads. The entire concept seems even less sane when one considers that most automobiles, according to a 1972 Department of Transportation study, are driven to ferry around not three or four motorists but 1.7 individuals: Americans do not like to be herded, yet their search for motorized elbow room is doomed to failure. There is only so much land, so much space for roadways . . .

Unless.

Motorcycles, again, can be saviors. The biggest motorcycle made, the Harley-Davidson Electra Glide, weighs in at less than 950 pounds with a full gas tank and a two-hundred-pound rider. The lightest American car made is the Ford Pinto runabout, which weighs two thousand pounds empty of both passenger and gas. An automobile will put more wear on the road than a bike will. . . . Hawaii might be the first state to ratify legislation on limiting the number of automobiles allowed on the island at one time. In May, 1972, Governor John A. Burns signed a bill establishing a commission to study the problem in depth.

Eventually, and probably quite soon, motorcycles will, like automobiles before them, become the targets of pollution-control people who will leap upon the bikes' emissions—in spite of the fact that cycles emit damned little, particularly when compared to a Lincoln Continental. The two-strokes will be the first assaulted since their emission, at least, is visible. The gasoline and oil mixture used by such machines as Yamaha, Kawasaki, Benelli, and most dirt bikes, is more polluting than straight gas burning Hondas, Triumphs, and BSAs. But even then, it is almost negligible.

In terms of actual pollution of the air by emissions, the motorcycle again easily surpasses the automobile in controlling pollution. The amount of emission from an engine is in direct proportion to the displacement size of the engine, and it stands to reason that the smaller the engine, the smaller the emission. As if this weren't a conclusive enough factor, it has been demonstrated that a motor burning the majority of the fuel taken into the combustion chambers will actually produce less emission than an engine burning up a smaller percentage of the fuel. Again, cycles win out. They make better use of the intaken fuel than the overwhelming majority of internal-combustion engines. It's not unusual for a small cycle to be running within a few hundred revolutions per minute short of its maximum capacity, thereby burning whatever gasoline is taken into the engine. An automobile can run ten thousand miles without once being pushed to its peak power.

The car's gas consumption, in terms of actual combustion, is far less than any motorcycle made, and the pollution it produces is, therefore, far greater. Lastly, the horsepower to weight ratio is so much smaller in an automobile (the biggest Chevrolet Corvette weighs 3,400 pounds and is rated at 270 horsepowers, roughly one horsepower per 12.5 pounds; a Norton Commando weighs 395 pounds, is rated at sixty horsepowers or one horsepower per 6.5 pounds) than in a motorcycle that the cars, under more load, naturally emit more gases.

If ever—and it is a possibility—a tax is imposed on emissions, a tax scaled to the amount of pollution produced by a motor vehicle, motorcycles will come out far ahead of even the minicars, and such behemoths as the Cadillac, the Imperial, and the "supercars" with massive engines will quite literally be legislated off the road, available to only a rich and gullible few who really think they require 365 cubic inches to do forty-five miles an hour.

From a strictly monetary point of view, an automobile is at best a poor investment. The initial outlay is anywhere from $2,000 to $25,000. With a few miles on it, even if new, the car is worth appreciably less. By the end of one year's driving, it has depreciated up to one-fourth or more. In a few years, it's virtually worthless. The upkeep, gasoline, and oil costs, repair bills, and tune-ups amount to a fair sum that increases in almost direct proportion to the original price and "luxury" of the car.

The Department of Transportation in a study made in May, 1972, found that a standard-sized automobile costs 13.6 cents per mile to operate, a compact costs 10.8 cents per mile, and a subcompact costs 9.4 cents a mile. A motorcycle is far cheaper to run, though admittedly a bit more complicated. An owner, capable of doing his own minor repairs and tune-ups, could ride a bike for approximately 5 cents a mile inclusive of original costs, insurance, gas, oil, tires, and registration taxes. The only setback to motorcycling, when all is accounted, is a lack of comfort and what to many seems an increased danger.

Bikes are more dangerous than automobiles, but their danger is a relative one, not so much initiated by the machine themselves as by inexperienced riders and blind automobiles. According to the Department of Transportation, the proportional injury rate of motorcycles is roughly nine times that of cars while the fatality rate is five times that of automobiles. Yet as a whole, bikers have proportionately fewer accidents than drivers.

The reason for this has not been determined. Some believe it's simply because less mileage is put on a bike than on a car during the course of a year. Others think motorcycle drivers, due to the very constant possibility of mishap, are far safer drivers.

A biker, open to the elements, is forced by his very lack of size and weight to drive far more defensively than a motorist. What to the family wagon is a scratch on the fender can well turn out to be a bad trip to the hospital for a cyclist. He therefore must depend on speed, reflexes, eyesight, and hearing to a far greater degree than virtually anyone else, and this must be tempered with the ability of being able to judge distances and anticipate other motorists' reactions. In the rain, his visibility and road holding are vastly diminished. The roads themselves are dangerous, offering potholes, oil slicks, sand, and other slippery surfaces to the unwary.

To his advantage are greater speed and quicker acceleration, better braking and handling than anything else on the roads. The greatest danger is not himself, it's the other man, a statement that has been proven by the motorcycle division of the California Highway Patrol. The CHP has logged eight million miles aboard bikes with only 175 accidents, all the more startling when you consider that the cops ride bikes year round, and they are as far removed from pleasure riding as any thing can be.

To all these facts should be added one of paramount importance. The past year has seen what has been dubbed an "energy crisis," one which has struck virtually every level of society from major companies to lowly individuals. Foreign relations political ineptness, and a lack of foresight which borders on downright stupidity have finally taken their toll.

The earth, we are told is slowly but inexorably running out of resources which mankind can plunder. This was brought home during the summer of 1973 when, for the first time, more than a few motorists suddenly found themselves short on gasoline, their local stations closed or limiting the supply of fuel to a set amount per customer. That this should strike the land of plenty would have been unthinkable a year ago, and is still not taken as seriously as it should be by most. We have all, certainly, been directly affected: the farmer whose farm machinery cannot work without gasoline, the station owner forced to roll up or roll back his prices, diminishing either his sales or his profits, the smaller oil companies faced with sudden and total bankruptcy.

Americans, by nature inveterate consumers, are now faced with a major problem: what do we do with the Caddy, the Imperial, the huge Oldsmobile sitting in the garage, the one which gets ten or twelve miles to the gallon? Americans are ambulatory creatures, whose way of life is based on quick travel from point A to point B, who commute insane distances in search of privacy, fun, work, peace and cheaper living. Motorcycles, again, might furnish the answer. A large bore bike gets 30 or more miles per gallon, a smaller one can get up to a hundred miles per gallon. The cost of running two large American cars for one year will buy a family motorcycle and maintain it. Perhaps this fact alone will change motorcycling from a hobby practiced by a minority to an accepted means of transportation for many.

In 1885, a German, Gottlieb Daimler, bolted together a small gasoline engine, two wheels, and a massive wooden frame to make the world's first internal-combustion-powered motorcycle. It wasn't all that good-looking.

The Indian, a venerable hunk of iron and steel, a restorer's dream. Few Indians are found in such good shape, and this one is the result of months of searching for parts and mechanical knowledge. It's worth over $2,500.

There was, naturally, no suspension or gearing, no rubber tires or brakes. It suspiciously resembled a wooden horse or a medieval torture machine.

In 1972, 233 different models manufactured by forty-three companies were available in the United States alone, discounting specialty machines or rare and priceless antiques hoarded by collectors. The growth and development of motorcycles wasn't as fast as that of automobiles or airplanes, but it's still a pretty impressive achievement when one considers that it took less than one hundred years. Daimler's experimental ugly duckling was the forerunner of both later automotive and motorcycling developments, developments that grew, then halted, for all good purposes, until the mid-fifties when the Japanese, still suffering from a faltering afterwar economy that prohibited the construction of automobiles, decided to put a little life in the industry.

The most complex machinery now on the road, and some say the most sophisticated sold to the general public, is without a doubt Japanese. The past three years have seen incredible advancements in suspension, engineering, and research, which have totally surpassed the efforts of the rest of the world.

The British and Germans virtually had not advanced since the war when they produced big four-stroke twins and singles that thumped and leaked their way merrily down the road. The Americans, in what can only be called American fashion, had opted for sheer size and weight, producing machines over 1,000 c.c. that weighed a ton and cornered like potatoes. The Italians seemed to have given up engine development in favor of chassis and gas-tank design and improvements in already flaming paint jobs. Which left a huge slice of the market to whomever could develop a good and inexpensive mode of transportation, one which did not leak or require too much attention. The British, Italians, Americans, Germans, and French could have done it rather simply, having stored a vast amount of technological knowledge. They were far ahead of whatever country might wish to get into the game and wipe it off the competitive slate. The fact that they didn't remains somewhat of a mystery.

Perhaps the thought that, after all, they did seem to have the market sewn up influenced their decision to stay in their technological stone age while the Japanese were playing with high-winding two-strokes and rotary valves. Another reason might have been the inherent conservatism of the larger companies who had been doing it thusly for so many years that their foresight had been blinded, or simply that they refused to invest the money necessary to researching and retooling.

Regardless of the reasons involved, the major companies, toward the end of the fifties and beginning of the sixties, found themselves faced with a difficult choice: stay with the models that they had been producing for several years and hope that the small-bike boom might be just a fad or start putting out smaller models to compete with the Japanese imports. They chose to hang on until the fad passed. It didn't. While Japanese machines swept the market, taking buyers away, European and American sales held steady, rose slightly but never did manage to catch up. The results were foreseeable. The Japanese reinvested their money to come forth with better-looking, faster, and more reliable machinery, got into racing, and proceeded to wipe out everybody else (in 1972, seventeen of the first twenty places in the Daytona Junior one-hundred-mile race went to Japanese machinery, and Yamaha won all twenty first places in the 250 junior/expert race. It was all very embarrassing). Both pro and amateur road and trail action is dominated now by Japanese machinery: Honda, still number one, being chased by Yamaha, and Suzuki and Kawasaki battling for third. The machines available are by no means perfect, yet do not have the bitchy temperament of European cycles. Honda has now three four-cylinder machines, monsters of reliability that will assuredly whittle off another share of Harley-Davidson and BMW's market. Kawasaki chose to go the super-bike route, producing three and eventually four frighteningly fast three-cylinder machines made to eclipse the best that Norton, BSA, Triumph, and Harley have to offer. Suzuki has chosen to stress dependability and is often associated with big, speedy bikes. Yamaha dominates the Japanese dirt-bike market, making several machines that cost far less and are as a rule more dependable and easier to repair than what Europe has to offer.

In a sense, there seems to be no future, for machines are already fast both in top speed and acceleration. The market does not need more speed, since it's by and large utterly useless, and it certainly doesn't need more motorcycles. Small companies are opening and going bankrupt both here and abroad, while large companies threaten to destroy both themselves and their customers by following the "Detroit" principle of automotive philosphy—build a new one every year and saturate. . . .

What then? The overwhelming danger to motorcycling is adverse legislation that might turn the machines from lithe and fast vehicles to things with straps, belts, pads, engine guards, and pollution devices. At that point, the industry will fold, for it will be unable to deliver what riders want. Prices will soar, as will weight, and the motorcycle will no longer be what it claims to be. Chances are, then, that most manufacturers will start developing bikes with built-in safety devices ahead of the legislation, and bikes will pollute less yet offer the same thrill as the earlier models.

The trend is already set. In 1973, motorcycles were built with standardized controls, all machines having the brakes, clutch, and shifting levers on the same side. They now almost all have sealed-beam headlights, and Harley-Davidson, Norton, Kawasaki, Yamaha, and Honda have on several models opted for front or rear-wheel disc brakes, more sensitive, accurate, and less apt to fade than regular internal mechanisms. A number of machines have Kill buttons placed within reach in case of throttle-linkage failure. Suspension and frame geometry have been bettered, as have the comfort hassles: vibrations, handlebar reach, and seat design. . . .

There's no doubt that small machines will get faster, and it's within reason to hope for over one hundred miles per hour 125 c.c. motorcycles and over eighty miles per hour 50 c.c. Someone, eventually, will come up with a perfect bike: one capable of handling street and dirt with equal verve, speed, and handling. Perhaps this machine will have an adjustable frame to regulate wheel base and height and a bicycle-like derailleur system to vary the gear ratios. Someone, too, will come out with a decent "factory" chopper, much like Detroit's supercar. Both Harley and Norton have already tried but failed miserably.

As of this writing, the big Japanese companies are in the throes of a bloody and costly cubic centimeter/horsepower battle which has all but wiped the British firebreathers from the market.

The creation of the four-cylinder 750 c.c. Honda, long rumored to exist

Sidecar racing, from its early days, has been far more popular in Europe than in America.

in the dark recesses of Sochiro's warehouses, was but the opening shot. The Honda Motor Company had struck the first, highly successful blow which stunned the opposition, but rival Japanese manufacturers were not long in presenting to the public amazing wonders of engineering. Yamaha, a year after Honda's 750s hit the street, had a 650 c.c. which strangely resembled Triumph's Bonneville and Tigers. Kawasaki, not to be outdone, put out a 750 c.c. three cylinder two-stroke which to this day is the fastest mass production machine available. So Yamaha put out a twin 750 c.c., said to be vibrationless (it isn't) and Suzuki released its secret weapon, a 750 c.c. water-cooled two-stroke twin.

The Europeans, startled, painted their machines different colors. It didn't do too much for sales, and BSA went under. BMW, the Bavarian monolith, upped its machines from 650 c.c. to 750 c.c. to 850 c.c., to close to 1,000 c.c. Norton went from 750 c.c. to 850 c.c. and the only European company to make some headway was, strangely enough, Moto Guzzi, largely unknown before the creation of its 750 c.c. and 850 c.c. transversal twins. Harley-Davidson cleaned up the sportster, but maintained its ridiculously high price and kept selling to people who would buy HD products anyway. Kawasaki, in a masterful coup, put out a four-cylinder 900 c.c. four-stroke, insuring sales to both two- and four-stroke fans. Kawasaki's four-cylindered monster has added new impetus to the battle.

The Japanese, long wary of invading Harley territory with anything bigger than a 750 c.c., have now, it's rumored, decided to wage war in earnest with the first though certainly not last, skirmish to be launched by Sochiro Honda. Japanese sources claim that nothing short of a 1,600 c.c. motorcycle is now being tested by Honda technicians, and that the machine will be released in late 1974 or early 1975. The machine, designed more as a long-distance tourer than as a road-burner, will try to steal both Harley and BMW customers with its claim of being the "Rolls Royce" of motorcycling, a term milked dry by Berliner Motor Company, long-time importers of Norton, Ducati, and BMW. Other Japanese manufacturers, while not overtly trying to match Sochiro's thunder, are preparing a virtually undefeatable line of bikes, singles, twins, triples, and multis, which threaten to once and for all chase most big Limey and Italian twins off the North American continent.

Yamaha has a four-stroke twin 500 c.c. and soon will have a 660 c.c. rotary twin Suzuki, preferring to remain water-cooled, will introduce a smaller 500 c.c. version of their 750 c.c. twin while Kawasaki is readying a 750 c.c. version of their best-selling 900 c.c.

And in the midst of the fighting, while Honda, Yamaha, Suzuki, and Kawasaki engage in their escalating free-for-all, someone will sneak in a Wankel-powered motorcycle which just might wipe out the opposition.

The ads say Wankel-engined cars go mmmmmmmmm while four-strokes go "twang-sputter." It's a simplistic explanation of what will soon be a revolution in motorized transportation. The Wankel engine, at the moment, probably holds the key to the future of internal-combustion engines, and the strange-looking triangular piston used in the rotary motors may well prove to be the four- and two-stroke engines' executioner.

The concept isn't new. In 1926, a German engineer and inventor by the name of Felix Wankel decided to explore the various possibilities of rotary engines, obtained a contract from the German NSU automotive firm,* and some years later, developed a prototype engine. In 1965, the NSU Spider became the first mass-produced Wankel-engined vehicle, to be followed by the Toyo Kogyo Mazda RX-2 and RX-3, which was recently introduced into the U.S. Today, rumors abound concerning the possible creation by American automotive interests of an American-built Wankel vehicle.

The Wankel engine is far simpler than its four-stroke brother. Three small chambers of variable size undergo one complete four-stroke cycle in one revolution of the triangular piston. The engine has no valves, the ports are opened and closed by the piston itself, and since the crankshaft makes three rotations for every one rotation of the triangular piston, the machine develops one power stroke for each rotation of the crankshaft, or twice the power stroke of the four-stroke engine. This means that for equivalent horsepower, a Wankel engine is about half the size and weight of a conventional two- or four-stroke. The simplicity of the engine is demonstrated by the fact that a standard 195 horsepower V-8 has 388 moving parts while its Wankel brother of the same power has only 154 moving parts. Reliability and doubled horsepower for the same weight and price. No vibrations, since the thing isn't reciprocating, more torque with lower octane fuels, less noise, better speeds, fuel economy, and low pollution.

The first of what will probably be a horde of Wankel-powered machines

---

* The firm's main interest in rotaries was to develop a workable valve mechanism and compressor that might be used in motorcycles.

THE MAZDA WANKEL ENGINE

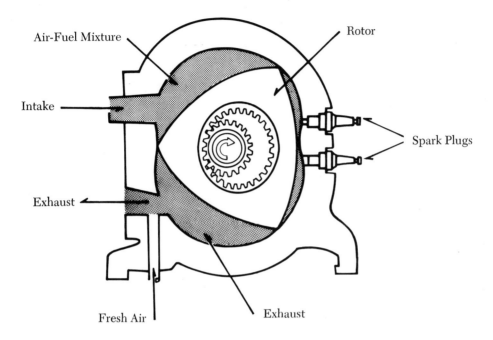

Air-Fuel Mixture

Rotor

Intake

Spark Plugs

Exhaust

Fresh Air

Exhaust

Diagram courtesy Mazda Motors

is already available in Germany. Costing close to $1,200, the Hercules W-2000's futuristic appearance matches its performance. It's a 250 c.c. road-bike with what looks like an air-conditioning unit placed below a double loop frame. Advertisers claim it can travel with virtually no vibrations at speeds in excess of 100 miles per hour.

In the spring of 1974, Suzuki is scheduled to bring out a Wankel machine of undetermined c.c.'s. Two other Japanese companies, Honda and Yamaha, are said to be experimenting with rotary-engine bikes.

The Wankel's engineering breakthroughs will probably take some time to be accepted in the States. American bikers are attached to their noisy and complicated twins and multis, perhaps not realizing that the shining machines they so proudly stride are but gilded relics. The four-stroke engine, after all, is all of ninety-seven years old, and for all its illustrious history, slated to be replaced.

6

Caveat Emptor
and Thieves in the Night

The legend is whispered at night, spread by word of mouth at motorcycle tracks, custom shows, dealer display rooms, club meetings, outlaw runs. The word is that there's a veritable El Dorado of old motorcycles and spare parts, all new, still wrapped in the original cosmoline and wax paper, a treasure trove of pre-1950 Harleys and Indians, springer front ends and rare rigid frames, cylinders, crankcases, heads, pistons. . . . They've never been used, never even started, and are in mint condition, left over from the time the government ordered too much and used too little. And they're practically giving them away. They're being sold for $50 apiece but you can buy them only in lots of ten or fifteen at once, so if every man puts $50 in the kitty, and we mail it to this address, quickly, because they're running out and there won't be any left in a couple of months. . . .

Every year, the people who handle the Armed Forces Surplus sales regretfully return a few thousand dollars to motorcycle clubs and hopeful dealers around the country all hoping to make a killing from the bikers' impossible dream. But some cyclists are less lucky and deal with individuals whose financial honesty is not quite that of military people, good old-fashioned con men who have found in the motorcycle boom a brand-new way to make a quick and effortless buck. The money sent in by the Oskeego Road Turtles for the ten 1948 Harley 1,200s disappears. So do the con men. The clubs are victims of what is in knowledgeable circles called the royal shaft or, more commonly, the rip off.

If there's a sucker born every minute, there's undoubtedly a gullible cyclist ripped off every day, from the purchase of his cut-rate racing leathers that split at every seam during the very first race to the repair of his machine by an unscrupulous mechanic. Cyclists, possibly, are gifted by that remarkable optimism that pinpoints what the carnies call the "mark," the one willing to be stripped of all his cash at a moment's notice, the man who'll purchase sight unseen anything from a one-of-a-kind motorcycle to a swamp lot in Florida and, unwilling to admit he's been taken, do it again one month later. The amount of money reaped yearly by fast-talking salesmen of doubtful reputation, by unscrupulous mail-order houses, and discount dealers cannot be counted. It runs in the hundreds of thousands of dollars.

Every fad, every boom, every momentary whim, and, later, every necessity is good fodder for twilight entrepreneurs who are ruthless in their capitalizing, selling defective or poorly constructed merchandise usually at fairly cheap prices. Some are discovered and put out of business, only to spring back a few days later with a brand-new name and a brand-new company selling the same trash to the same public. Others go on forever, draining every last penny from an affluent market. Since there is no quality control, no exchange or refunds, and no aftersale servicing in many facets of buying and selling, it's relatively easy to show a good, quick profit from a *caveat emptor* organization.

Since motorcycling is a relatively new sport and hobby in the United States, many buyers rarely know what they're getting into when they purchase that first machine, all paint and reflected sunlight. The reputable dealers will give a short course in motorcycling mechanics, realizing that a satisfied customer is likely to come back for the purchase of a second, bigger bike. But a lot of dealers show absolutely no regard for the biker's safety. The machine, once off the showroom floor, is no longer the seller's responsibility. The buyer is suddenly on his own, and all the advertising that claims his new Kawaguchi is fast, reliable, and handles like rubber cement is of no help getting around the curve, trying to figure out how the hell you stop it from wheelieing at every red light and which button does what to what.

When motorcycling was even newer to these shores than it presently is, storefront peddlers blossomed like acne, selling unheard-of machines for lower prices than the top ten. With demand high, predelivery preparations were cursory at best, and bikes were handed over to joyous customers with scarcely more than a half-hearted attempt to tighten down bolts that looked obviously too loose, inflate the tires, and fill up with gas and oil. It was not uncommon to purchase a bike, drive it home, and suddenly be passed by the rear wheel, which had come off, or listen incredulously to the clanking and gnashing of a chain as it exited via a primary cover, leaving an obscenely large hole in the polished aluminum.

Repairs on many of the early machines imported to the States—Marusho, Tohatsu, Gilera, Parilla, Benelli—were rarely made properly. Parts were scarce or nonexistent, and the dealers, established in a hurry to rake in the money before the fad faded, had little if any knowledge of elementary mechanics. The rider could shake his head and moan, curse, and wail to no avail.

Lest it be thought that only the smaller companies had this kind of problem, it should be mentioned that even the Big Four—Honda, Yamaha, Kawasaki, and Suzuki—were often as guilty as their smaller competitors. The first Japanese machines imported had their own little quirks and hangups, and parts were not to be found. Repair work was shoddy, if that good, and dealers far too anxious to push their product with little care for anything beyond the customers' money. The manufacturers were even guiltier, for, in their haste to flood the market, they created hundreds of models, shipped them out, and sold them with no thought of inventory. Honda, in a scant five years, put out more than one hundred different motorcycle models, and, in some areas, it was impossible in 1972 to find parts for 1970 motorcycles that had been discontinued. Ordering parts direct from Japan is a joke, and the dealers themselves cannot be faulted for their lack of inventory. One long-established dealer in Maryland waited eighteen months for a $2 part to arrive, and, by his own accounting, exchanged thirty-seven different letters, order forms, and part descriptions with his Japanese distributor.

It is, as a rule, far safer to deal with a long-established dealer of good reputation than save a few dollars in a hole-in-the-wall shop. Some dealers are good, some are bad, some are legendary for their dishonesty. The latter generally don't last, but it doesn't take too many high-paying customers to keep a thief in business. Riders, luckily, are a cliquish lot, quick to pass the word that SO-and-SO is a cheating S.O.B. so stay away from him. The best advice a cyclist can follow, when it comes to dealing with unknown bike shops, is public opinion. Seeking out other bikers with previous experience can save much money and aggravation. The problems encountered by motorcyclists in need of repair for their vehicles are much the same as those encountered by car drivers. There's not much of a line of defense, particularly since good bike-repair shops are scarcer than hen's teeth, and comparison shopping is impractical. Mechanics' fees can range from $5 to $12, and while, again, the majority of bike mechanics are honest, enough aren't to make the average rider suspicious of any and all repairs on his machine.

Ask for a complete estimate before the work is done, request all old parts removed and replaced, ask for a rundown and itemization of the work done. This is no guarantee that you won't get ripped off, but if you're going to get cheated, at least make the man work for it. The opinion of other riders can also be helpful when it comes to buying accessories by mail. In the past five years, mail-order houses catering to custom motorcyclists have flourished and are now making a ludicrous amount of money. Leafing through a chopper magazine the reader will be inundated with ads for chopper parts of unknown quality and highly competitive prices. Differentiating the honest from the dishonest is time-consuming and costly. Again, it's best to deal with a well-known company whose integrity has been proven. Some parts now offered for sale should be avoided if one is anxious to keep head and body together, for these accessories are not only a rip off, they're deadly.

When the chopper fad started sweeping California, bright boys in search of the "long, lean look" discovered that a lot of money could be saved by inserting long slugs into the forks, and a fly-by-night "slug industry" was created, furnishing metal cylinders up to one foot long. The slugs, if properly installed, could last but generally did not. They broke, and at high speeds this was enough to throw the rider several feet into the air. As slugs became unpopular, entire front end assemblies were sold for prices ranging from $100 to $300. These were safer, but prone to metal fatigue and breakage under severe stress. Some developed high-speed flexing or wobbling.

Stroking and boring kits that increased the displacements of motorcycle engines were sold with no thought of safety to riders wanting more power for less money than the price of a new bike. These kits were prone to seizure and sometimes stressed the bottom end of the engine to the breaking point. Custom gas tanks leaked. "Genuinely stitched motorcycle seats" fell apart. Exhaust systems rusted away; high rpm camshafts disintegrated right in the engine. Mail-order "engine rebuilding houses" scarcely looked at the engines sent them. They cleaned them up, and sandblasted motor covers to make them look new, then sent them back to delighted customers who swore they could "feel the difference."

Perhaps the most wanton disregard manifested by mail-order houses was the sale of inexpensive helmets about as protective to the rider as a paper party hat. These helmets were simply a plastic shell lined with foam rubber and supplied with a canvas webbing made to "cushion" shocks. Since recent legislation in many states now requires that cycle helmets be approved by an impartial testing agency, the sale of these cheap replicas has somewhat diminished, though they can still be found in many surplus stores and discount houses.

Approximately 250 motorcycles are stolen daily in the United States; 25 percent of these are recovered, in varying degrees of mechanical health, and the rest vanish along a well-established underground railroad of hot bikes and hot parts. If one takes the average worth of each motorcycle ridden down the road at $700 (an optimistically low average, particularly since the trend seems headed toward bigger and more expensive machines), the amount of money lost to the nation's estimated six million riders comes to some $63 million.

Motorcycle theft is now an organized crime where orders for a particular model are taken and the motorcycle furnished at half price, where black market rates will bring in up to $200 for the title of a wrecked and irreparable large bore machine. There are professional gangs of thieves who roam the streets at night equipped with bolt cutters, chain hoists, and vans. It takes less than thirty seconds for an experienced team to hoist or roll a motorcycle into a panel truck and drive away. In less than a week, the stolen machine will either have been completely repainted and sold (with another motorcycle's title) or stripped down, the parts disseminated to various buyers with hard cash. Either way, the bike is gone for good. The police auhorities are hard put to retrieve bikes. The large majority of cops (motorcycle cops included) have no training in distinguishing one machine from another. A Honda 500 looks enough like a Honda

750 c.c., which, if you don't know your bikes, looks like a BSA 3. A machine's appearance can be radically changed by switching gas tanks and seats, and a stolen bike could be ridden right in front of its original owner without being recognized. Bikes are easy to steal, and easy to hide. They have, according to *Cycle World* magazine, been found in Los Angeles hotel closets and, according to police, have been discovered in basements, bedrooms, and outhouses. The record theft was probably pulled off in France when three American Harley-Davidson 1200 c.c. motorcycles were recovered from an aged widow's attic.

The rise of motorcycle theft hits the average rider directly in the wallet, even if his personal machine is not ripped off.

Insurance companies find themselves in a quandary. The rates they must charge for theft coverage are downright outrageous, and unfortunately necessary if they're to keep their heads up in a money-making society. A large number of companies have simply stopped writing theft policies for motorcycles, others are turning down renewals, leaving the biker with his $3,000 custom machine and no protection. Worse, perhaps, is the fact that dealers increasingly have to demand cash for new machines. Credit corporations have learned that a man whose uninsured machine has been ripped off will be less than delighted to keep up the payments. Joseph E. Bloggs in a *Cycle World* magazine feature stated that the loss rate in Massachusetts and New Jersey borders at 200 percent, which in layman's terms means that an insurance company operating in these two states must pay out $200 for every $100 premium collected.

But if the world at large seems to be composed of scavengers waiting behind every lamppost, armed with heavy-duty chain cutters and master keys, it should be added that the cyclists themselves sometimes add to the problem. Insurance companies must deal with what is termed the "friendly" rip off.

A cyclist insures his machine heavily. A friend "steals" it, hides it overnight in his garage, and the theft is reported by the owner to police authorities. The police shrug their shoulders and say they'll do the best they can. A few weeks later, when the theft of the cycle is a number in the back of someone's file drawer, the biker and his friend dump the machine, or bury it, or, occasionally, sell it out of state without a title (particularly dirt machines that often need not be registered) and collect their righteously claimed payment from the insurance company.

It's all very depressing to the average owner with no larcenous thoughts in the back of his head, a very bleak picture indeed. . . . Yet the average cyclist is not totally at the mercy of the thief if he understands and applies a few basic principles.

There are primarily two types of thieves operating—the casual joy rider and the professional; both want your machines, but for vastly different reasons. The joy rider will look and want it temporarily, until something better comes up or simply until the thrill of riding it is gone. The professional's motives are entirely different. The machine, in his eyes, is a financial investment that, for the time spent in acquisition, will give satisfactory returns. His outlook on the theft is generally cold and unemotional, merely practical. Knowing the psychology of thieves can help deter a theft.

The joy rider will hop on the machine and ride it away, if his risks are minimal. A chain, or a simple fork lock, can dampen the enthusiasm of the moment. Any hindrance, no matter how simple, might take his attention from your machine to someone else's. The professional will come well-armed, and quite ready, if necessary, to invest more than one evening's work into getting your bike.

The best theft deterrent is a hefty, case-hardened chain with a good lock. Chained through the frame, a machine is immovable. The chain should be placed high enough to prevent leverage for the bolt cutters. It shouldn't be chained to a small tree or anything easily removable. Small trees, stop signs, and porch railings have been cut before and will be again. Any number of small, imaginative tricks will also work. Switch the sparkplug leads or fit a dud spark plug. Put a matchbook cover between the points of your engine. Remove the baffles from the mufflers, and the thief, with luck, will be picked up by the cops.

Use a fair amount of common sense. Park in a well-lit area, where the machine can be seen. If you have friends who also own bikes, make a deal and chain the lot of them together. No thief, no matter how ambitious, will try to rip off three or four BMWs at once.

There are several excellent alarms available. The best of the lot are put out by Security Products Division in Mt. Laurel, New Jersey. Cycle Guard I consists of a thin black box on which is mounted the cycle's license plate. Inside the box is a beeping unit activated by a mercury switch. If the machine is moved, it starts screaming like a banshee, then stops after a couple of minutes. If someone tries to move the bike again or ride it away, the alarm keeps on screaming merrily for hours, providing unwanted attention. Cycle Guard II is the same as Cycle Guard I with added sophistication. There's a small radio-sending unit in the little black box, and you're furnished with a pocket receiver that, even if the alarm is out of hearing range, will beep. The mercury switches are adjustable.

Their main drawbacks are two. Virtually anything can set the alarm off. A kid accidentally hitting your machine, a strong wind, a slight nudge. The alarm owner thinking of doing a half gainer down the elevator shaft to get to his beeping cycle in the parking lot might end up nose to nose with a cop trying to find a place to put a parking ticket. And the Cycle Guard units, particularly the radio-equipped one, are expensive, slightly under $90 for Cycle Guard II and $35 for Cycle Guard I. Their purchase, however, is enough to deter most thieves. A chain and an alarm make an almost unbeatable combination, as the thief will have to move the machine if only to cut the chain. One deterrent works with the other.

One of the most common subjects of conversation between bikers is So-and-So's purchase of an almost brand-new Norton Commando S from a little old man who rode it to the grocery store every Sunday to get a bag of fresh bagels. So-and-So bought it for next to nothing, a real steal, and he's been riding it ever since. . . .

Cyclists are ripped off every year buying used machines from little old men and little young men, brand-new machines with five hundred miles, never raced, never blown up, or wrecked. Harleys and Triumphs always driven twenty miles an hour, shiny beasts with low price tags and brand-new tires.

The used-motorcycle market has boomed as fast as the new one, particularly in America where change is the order of the day, where new machinery renders the old obsolete before the rust sets in, where wealth is equated with annual turnover. Any large city newspaper will advertise virtually every make and model of motorcycle, every displacement, color, and style. To the uninitiated, buying a used machine might seem wise, the obvious thing to do. Why pay twice the price for a new one, particularly when the used one looks just as good, makes the same sound, and is already broken in?

The basic and uncomfortable thing to remember about used motorcycles is that most of the time people sell them simply because they don't like them. There are basically three stock answers to "Why are you selling it?": (1) "I'm getting something bigger," (2) "I need the money to go to college/

to leave college/to buy a car," (3) "My girl friend/wife/mother/father/ daughter/mistress/neighbor doesn't like it." The answers, however, vary with the imagination of the seller, and prospective buyers have heard such unforgettable ones as: "It's too big, I just can't handle it" . . . "You're bigger than I am, maybe you've got more guts," and "Well, I just bought this Honda 160 to prove to the guy next door that I could wipe out his Norton in the quarter mile, and now I did it, so I don't really need the machine anymore." Chances are the reasons given for the sale are not quite as honest as they should be.

A motorcycle, regardless of its displacement or bulk, has in reality very little in common with an automobile: the engine might or might not be of the same design, and, like a car, a motorcycle rolls. But all in all, it's a different breed of beast, a fact that must be considered. When a motor vehicle of 750 c.c. can outspeed and outaccelerate another vehicle of eight times its engine size, turn higher rpms and lower times at a drag strip, and generally do everything better than a car, elementary facts like engine stress and wear, engine time and mileage must be taken into account. A car will perhaps once or twice during its short life operate at maximum capacity, flat out, accelerator to the floor in fourth gear. Some automobiles will never even undergo such a minor strain, their owner content to loll along, using a maximum 40 percent of the engine's potential. A motorcycle is another story.

A Honda red-lined at twelve thousand revolutions per minute should not be run at much lower than 3/4 engine speeds. Lugging a motorcycle engine, aside from being uncomfortable, is quite harmful. The average engine speed of a motorcycle is approximately 2/3 of its total potential. It's not unusual to run a bike as hard as it can be run (particularly the machines with smaller engines) for long periods of time. The rate of attrition is therefore far higher than a car's ever is. Pistons are replaced with fair frequency. A top end will see as many as ten valve jobs, an engine might be overhauled totally more than four times. An automobile will get one valve job in its lifetime, and many an automobile has not been honored by a total overhaul before being towed off to rust in some suburban junkyard. A motorcycle must be in at least good tune even to run properly, and it will wear out in direct relation to its upkeep.

From the outside, it's impossible to tell what shape a bike is in. It probably will not be old enough to be judged by exterior appearance, as many machines are kept shiny and polished even if the engine is a mess. Motor-cycle sounds differ greatly, and only a professional can fully diagnose an engine's ills by listening to it. Steering and road holding differ from one machine to another. An oil leak in a British machine is to be expected, since their bikes have a tendency to leave great pools of various fluids wherever they go. The same problem in a Japanese machine might be far more serious, as the Japanese build virtually air- and oil-tight cases. Two-stroke motor-cycles will smoke profusely if maladjusted and not quite as profusely if well-tuned. A four-stroke should not smoke, period.

The obvious thing to do, then, is stay away from used machines. Their price does not justify the subsequent problems too often encountered, the hassles and headaches that warrant trips to unsympathetic dealers. A new machine with a dealer's warranty is worth the extra dollars involved, even if it isn't as big a bike as you originally thought of buying. But if you are in the market for a used motorcycle, there are several things a buyer can check to insure an acceptable deal before laying down his money.

Unless you're an expert, with a motorcycle shop and all the knowledge and two or three thousand dollars' worth of tools necessary to do good work on a machine, bring a friend who (1) has the same machine as you plan to buy or (2) knows more about it than you do. Then go out and ride a new model of the bike you're interested in, or, if unavailable, the nearest thing to it. Remember the machine's characteristics. Start with the idea that the man selling you the machine is probably ready and willing to lie and slander and cheat to get you to buy, then don't let him. Let the machine speak for itself.

As a rule of thumb, an ill-cared-for machine, full of scratches and rust, will probably be as scarred on the inside as it is on the outside. Frayed cables, bent levers, torn seats, and loose nuts and bolts show a general lack of care, which will probably be magnified on internal components.

General Once-over

Look at the machine, turn a deaf ear to its owner and smile and nod as he tells you what's right with it. Sit on the machine, decide whether it's com-fortable, whether your feet and hands reach the levers. Squeeze the levers. If they're too soft or too hard, ask why. See if the throttle snaps back. Don't trust speedometers. They can be disconnected or simply changed. And they're incredibly optimistic. Many a machine incapable of doing better than eighty miles per hour will have a speedometer going up to 120 miles per hour. Check the chain. If the adjustors on the rear of the swing arm are all the way back and the chain can be stretched vertically more than three-quarters of an inch, chances are you'll have to buy a new one in short order. Check the teeth on the rear-wheel sprocket. Are they worn too much, or unevenly? Are the adjustors on the clutch and brake levers all the way out? Rest the bike on the center stand and have your friend sit on the rear wheel so the front wheel is off the ground. If the forks seem to be loose on the frame, you'll probably need new bearings or worse. Spin the front wheel. It should spin freely, and placing yourself directly in front of it and squinting with one eye should be enough to see whether it's out of line. Hold a pencil perpendicular to the rim and spin the wheel again, this time to see that the rim itself hasn't been bashed up. Bikes with disk brakes might have slightly binding front wheels, but should still be aligned. Run your fingers under the machine's engine and see if they come out covered with greasy stuff. Check the engine covers and tailpipes for telltale marks of accidents. Deep scratches and gouges mean the bike has probably been dumped. Check the electrics, particularly on British bikes. The English have for years been relying on Lucas electric components, which always seem to conk out at the wrong moment. If the circuits and wirings are in good shape, the intensity of the lights should increase slightly when the machine is revved up. Check the tires to see whether they're unevenly worn, and if they are, check the wheels again. Crank it over, just to see if the machine has the compression it should have. Take the spark plugs out and check them. Touch the cylinders and see if they're warm, which would mean that the bike was run just before you came and will therefore be easier to start If you have time, wait for the cylinders to cool down, then start the machine.

Riding the Bike

Don't buy a machine that the owner will not let you or your friend ride. It's too easy for him to minimize the defects that he knows about and can avoid while you're riding on the buddy seat. Start the machine. Check the idle and check, if it's a twin or multi, that one cylinder doesn't lag behind the other. Check the smoke from the exhausts and see whether anything drips oil when running, whether the wheels turn when the bike is in neutral.

Listen to the engine noises. If the bike jingles or makes gnashing noises, ask why and don't take "They all do that" for an answer. Does the machine jump around on its center stand? Old Nortons, renowned for their bone-loosening vibrations, did little dances and could hop half a block while idling, but newer machines whose engines are well-balanced shouldn't go anywhere. Drive the cycle at least two or three miles, through curves, good roads and bad roads, over a couple of potholes and ruts, and in all gears, wind it out from bottom to top, and check if there are any lags or backfires in the engine, any flat spots in the acceleration. Does the bike break loose during tight curves or shimmy? Does it have a high- or low-speed wobble? Does the clutch engage smoothly? Ride it to thirty-five or forty miles an hour and brake with both brakes. Do it four or five times and judge the amount of brake fade. There will be some, but the brakes should remain effective. Don't take any guff about the brakes working "after heating up." See that the front forks and rear shocks don't bottom out over bumps. If they do, you'll hear and feel it, and probably have to put in for a new suspension.

After the Ride

Go out and ride a few other machines of the same model. If none are for sale, deeply consider the fact that you might be getting a rare bird that no one will have parts for or know how to repair.

Be insulting and ask to check the frame numbers against the title, just to make sure you're not getting a hot bike. Ask why there are scratches there. If the seller stutters or blushes, or doesn't quite know what to say, leave quickly.

Now talk to the owner. He'll swear the machine has never been ridden down or in an accident or blown up. He might even be telling the truth. Don't buy it right away. Go home and think it over, mull the various things that you didn't like and couldn't understand. Get an outside opinion on why it might do what it does. Remember the investment you're making and, after due thought, decide either to buy it or not. Just to be mean and save a little money, offer the seller one-fifth less than he's asking. If he agrees with a look of relief on his face, take it for granted that you're still offering more than he thought he would get and give this idea some thought. With some luck, you might get what you see—or you might get ripped off. If you're a wise man, decide that, after all, you'd rather get a new machine and have the satisfaction of knowing nothing's been done to it yet.

Possibly more tempting than a "straight" machine are the multiple offers for choppers, raked and lowered beasties usually found under "Harley," "Chopper," or "Custom Cycle" in the classified ads. These are machines usually bought secondhand by the seller, who has added his personal touches to various frame, suspension, or engine components. Few things are more risky than buying a chopper, used, whose past history cannot be verified and on which several "experiments" have been performed. The great chopper fad has done many weird things to perfectly good motor-cycles, and the unfortunate side of the often handsome modifications is that most changes have been highly injurious to the basic safety of the machine. A frame that has been cut and reshaped will be weaker than a stock frame, often regardless of the care taken in rewelding. Overlong forks tend to lose their basic function and, past a certain size, will simply no longer work. Molded frames are beautiful, but will prove to be quite difficult to repair, and many chopper owners have sadly seen their Fiber-glas molding chip away after a few months on the road. The molding also complicates frame identification if the machine is ever stolen. Bikes to which "hard-ass" rigid frames have been bolted might look good, but do an outrageously poor job of road holding and take a certain amount of guts to ride more than a few hundred miles. Bikes without suspension are often vastly uncomfortable. The underlying fact is that such machines are too often amateurishly built monsters that will only go straight. The bolt-on-bolt-off school of motorcycling is hardly the safest, and too many choppers are only that, for all their good looks and clean lines. Buying a chopper can be a good investment if one is fully familiar with frame geometry, engine balancing, and various other technical aspects of mechanical lore. A new and inexperienced biker on a chopper is rolling death.

The final word concerns new machines. There are some ten best-selling motorcycle makes in the United States, and another ten to fifteen smaller companies putting out fairly specialized bikes designed for on- and off-road use. The quality of service has vastly improved during the past five years, but even the most honest dealers and stalwart manufacturers make mistakes. The majority of machines imported here undergo a battery of test runs at the home factory, since manufacturers now realize that exporting a dud might create immediate sales but will, in the long run, be highly detrimental to future exports and reputation. Aftersale service has also vastly improved, ever since both dealers and companies realized the sudden boom was not a fad but a steadily climbing market. Testing, though it does rid the machines of obvious kinks, often does not detect long-term effects of strain on some parts. First year machinery can sometimes be troublesome. The first Kawasaki Mach III, a three-cylinder two-stroke cycle that garnered kudos from riders and critics alike, developed a heating problem in the center cylinder. There were some seizures, some blown engines, and some disgruntled customers. The first Honda four-cylinder 750 c.c. machines were hailed as the greatest development in motorcycle history, which they were, until they were recalled twice, the first time voluntarily to repair sticky throttles and the second time with a bit of prodding from the Department of Transportation, the International Four-Owners Association, and *The Washington Post* newspaper after it was discovered that a weak main link in the chain had caused much discomfort to many Honda owners. The chain was wont to break at high speeds, possibly locking up the rear wheel and throwing the entire machine out of control. The Honda people in Gardena, California, were less than gracious about admitting the fault was theirs, preferring to attribute it to faulty maintenance by the owners.

In-house memos, made available to the press and the Department of Transportation by an ex-Honda executive, clearly revealed that Honda was aware of the problem, was concerned and did want to remedy it, but did not want to send out a general recall order. The problem was magnified by the fact that motorcycles switch hands far more often than automobiles, and there was no guarantee that all Honda-Four owners could be notified.

One problem encountered by many new bike buyers is the warranty that accompanies the sale. Generally cryptic, the dealers do little to really inform the buyers, and are generally quite unhappy about warranty work, which, after all, does not bring in a profit. Learn exactly what your warranty says. Early Honda-Four owners whose chains snapped took to replacing the chains themselves, thereby voiding whatever guarantee they had that Honda would bear the price of the often expensive repairs. But warranties have been voided by less. Some state that a biker may not do any work on his machine. Changing a blown light bulb is enough to void it, as is modifying the machine in any way. Such warranties can be so thorough as to work against the buyer, who, for a simple adjustment, might have to wait as long as a couple of weeks.

Make sure the machine has been put together properly. Motorcycles shipped overseas are generally received by the dealer in separate pieces and assembled at the dealer's shop by mechanics. It's not uncommon to buy a machine on which certain procedures have been overlooked in the assembly. Upon delivery of the bike, ride it a few miles and check out everything including chain tension and axle nuts, oil level in both tank and engine, making sure all grease fittings have been properly attended. If anything looks or feels unsatisfactory, tell the dealer about it before you take the beast home, and feel no shame in quibbling. When you're spending up to $2,000, you've got a right to question and it's easier to adjust various parts while you're still on the premises than it is to drive the bike home only to return it the next day.

Well-known machines are better bets than unheard-of ones, if only to be sure of aftersale service. It's good to remember that simple bikes are far safer for the inexperienced than exotic machinery needing constant care and adjustment, for, like the automobiles of our gadget age, the less there is, the less breaks down.

One last word concerning the most recent motorcycling fad to hit the States, namely the sidecar.

The sidecar, or hack as it's commonly called, was imported to America by economy-minded Europeans whose motorcycles were more family transportation than pleasure or sport vehicles. In America, it's still a fairly original mode of transportation, guaranteed to turn heads and elicit either jeers or compliments. Some consider them out and out bastardizations, caught somewhere between automobile and motorcycles, incapable of sweeping turns, more dangerous than two-wheelers and, as a rule, far trickier to handle. Others see them as the perfect solution for taking the family along.

A biker wishing to equip his beast with a third wheel should consider the matter carefully before spending the $400 to $800 required. Sidecars, fun though they may be, can present problems. The steering geometry is radically altered, and the three-wheeled bike is to be handled far differently from a two-wheeler. Braking will suffer, since the majority of hacks are not equipped with braking systems, handling and maneuverability are affected and the machine itself will probably need more upkeep and care, since it will be pulling at least an extra 150 pounds of dead weight.

Their advantage, however, cannot be discounted. Aside from the obvious fact that they provide more room, they make motorcycling far more stable in ice or snow and offer a comfortable and warm alternative to people suffering from two-wheel queasiness. Finally, they're just plain fun, once the rider is accustomed to their quirks, and open up new vistas, particularly for the touring rider.

There are several models presently available in the States, with prices roughly ranging from $320 for a "stripped-bare" model to over $1,000 for custom hacks, complete with stereo cassette, carpeting and windshield wiper.

7

Choppers and Beasties
That Roar in the Night

Saturday afternoon. There's a drag race on, and crowded into the too-small parking area sit dozens of vans, trailers, pick-up trucks. The machines being spent on the strip are lean, bare frames, wheels and engines devoid of all frivolities, and they go like bats out of hell, straight down the asphalt, smoking and crinkling the expensive Goodyear slicks. In one corner of the parking lot, generally placed conspicuously in full view of an admiring audience, rest the strip-machines' road brothers. Long, very, very lean, chromed and flowing in spotless paint jobs costing thousands of dollars—choppers. Big mean, S.O. Bitchin' machines.

The word itself seems evil, inherently murderous. It reeks of armpits and grease, gasoline and oil fumes, the distilled raunchiness of motorcycles pushed to the nth degree. Chops, scoots, representative of a flaunting disregard for even elementary safety; big, bright, and screaming at the Citizen Johns that they'll be run over but quick if they don't get the family Rambler out of the curve and onto the shoulder of the road. The beast might not have a front brake, and shouldn't have much of a suspension. It won't handle all that well, either, regardless of what the owner says. When you're being pushed along by 1,200 c.c. of hog power on a rigid frame with a little-functioning front end, you're not altogether that ready for hairpin curves.

The chopper is to cycles what the hot rod was to the automobile—the outlaw projection of home engineering; metal bullets that gun barrel down the road after the utterance of a small prayer to the patron saint of manufactured welding joints.

As virtually every other form of automotive expression beyond the pale and norm of everyday life, the chopper's background is debatable, and, as it is unlikely that anyone will ever write a history of these bastardized motorcycles, theories concerning their origins are many and varied.

Some say they are the product of the post-World War II money influx when young men returned from the battlefields and defense industries with money to burn or spend on outrageous ideas. Hence, a motorcycle was bought by a fellow with slightly baroque tastes in transportation. Since the said motorcycle, like most postwar vehicles, was staid, it probably failed to satisfy its owner, and American ingenuity aided by a welding torch and a few pounds of sheet metal was applied to the frame and gas tank. The result was often a motorcycle of questionable taste but unrivaled originality, a one-of-a-kind piece of machinery upon which any rider would be proud to sit, if not really ride.

Another theory suspects quite the opposite: young men, not as rich as they should be, purchased Army-surplus Harleys and Indians and applied Army-learned mechanics to weather-beaten engines, making the machines run, for a time, with renewed vigor. Since khaki colors, wide gas tanks, and monstrous fenders were never the height of wheeled fashions, a few days' work in neighborhood garages stripped the beasts of their more obnoxious accessories. Gas tanks, fenders, and thick, tubular front ends were replaced by skinnier and lighter British or homemade parts.

The two most popular theories, bandied about by a number of California chopper makers (who probably know what they're talking about), also date the creation of choppers to the mid and late forties. The first states that motorcycles, beginning to be a common sight among West Coasters, were often stolen by gang members to be sold for quick money. The bikes, once transported to a secret workshop, were made radically different, largely unrecognizable to their former owners, and peddled by fences for reduced prices. Serial numbers were shaved off and changed by gifted manipulators of hammer and dies, titles and license plates were acquired

But if you've got money, time, or talent, with the various different paints available today, you can opt for dots and gold leaf, as the owner of this Honda Four did. Chopper paint jobs are limited only by the imagination and financial abilities of the owners.

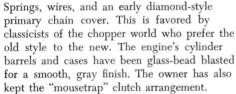

Springs, wires, and an early diamond-style primary chain cover. This is favored by classicists of the chopper world who prefer the old style to the new. The engine's cylinder barrels and cases have been glass-bead blasted for a smooth, gray finish. The owner has also kept the "mousetrap" clutch arrangement.

The other side of the chopper builder's art. "Longshot" is a radical show chopper, which started out as a Harley-Davidson. It features a girder front end, magnesium rear wheel, and paneling that almost covers the entire frame. "Longshot" is rarely ridden, but a constant show winner.

by stealth and conscientious bribery of minor Motor Vehicle Department officials. The other explains that drag racing, one of the only all-American racing inventions, is the father of all chops.

The men who tore up the quarter mile were imaginative and engineering, and their machines were awfully fast. The beasts could be made road-rideable, too, with the addition of slightly bigger gas tanks, lights, and other necessities. They could then be used on weekends to garner extra cash and sometimes trophies and still be used as a form of eye-catching transportation during the rest of the week.

Be it as it may, the chopper surfaced full-fledged in America sometime in the late forties, often ridden by small groups of young men who tried very hard and sometimes succeeded in frightening small towns. The machines were to suffer from an unsavory reputation for more than two decades until their metamorphosis from dragon to steed was brought about by Peter Fonda's *Easy Rider*.

For a number of years, the bigger and established chopper builders were virtually underground, often hassled by the local police, ticketed constantly for vehicle violations, and busted repeatedly for possession of stolen merchandise.

They were ignored by the populace at large, which had more than enough on its hands trying to subdue hot-rod gangs who traveled the land, and despised by the older motorcycle riders who were trying to make the motorcycle an accepted mode of transportation.

Motorcycle and hot-rod magazines refused their advertising. The builder's existence depended largely on the grapevines that always unite a tight group of people.

The Hell's Angels and other motorcycle rowdies in search of two-wheeled individuality rode choppers even then, which automatically made the machines the black sheep of cycledom. The American Motorcycle Association (AMA) decried their very existence and was quoted numerous times as saying that chopper riders and other cycle outlaws accounted only for 1 percent of all the North American riders. The venerable institution, up until a short time ago, had never really been held accountable for the statistics its public-relations men made, and chances are that even in the early fifties, more than 1 percent rode chopperized motorcycles. The great majority of that small percentage were simply riders with a taste for individuality, but enough were troublemakers to make an immediate association between motorcycles and violence almost mandatory.

It must be admitted, too, that the custom-bike people sometimes did little to alleviate their vehicle's infamy: if choppers were to imply sweaty armpits and obscene hand gestures, then so be it . . . raunchiness has always been a great American tradition. And if choppers were to represent war horses, again, so be it. The riders would be outlaws. One image reinforced the other, each increasing its strength. Riders discovered that they could scare people, and, more often than not with a "fun and games" mentality, did just that. The trouble was that the citizens didn't really relish fright, even in fun. A hobby's a hobby, but waking up the townsfolk at four in the morning and smashing the big plate-glass window of the local tavern is not all that humorous, even if, as was often done, the damage was paid in full after the night's revelry.

Times changed and so did the machines. As more experienced hands wielded more professional tools, and as more money was poured into increasingly extravagant machines, the conventional squatness of the early Harleys and Indians was melted or chiseled away, replaced by flowing curves that came to blend one into the other in quasi-harmonious relationships.

The idea was to have a moving projectile, a large hunk of sheer energy, tailored to fit the rider's need as well as his self-defined and self-enforced image.

If seen as such, choppers are not as outrageous as they might appear at first sight; there is a reason to their madness, a method to their engineering: their length is not accidental. It's there by design, by a weird coagulation of necessity and style. . . . California is a paved land, a heaven of unending expressways, straight as arrows and vanishing toward a distant if smoggy horizon. There are few turns, few tricky, winding hillside streets for the California city warrior to negotiate. Almost everything's straight, and the machine's wheelbase will be calculated accordingly. A short wheelbase will enable the cycle to handle rough terrain, a long one is perfect to handle curveless roads, and, additionally, far more comfortable; raked front ends allow the rider to lean back and relax, far more so than he could were he riding a stock machine.

The low seat and lack of suspension, too, are a product of the environment. A chopper rider will have no reason to venture from the paved roadways. Seldom will he encounter ruts or potholes for his surroundings are rectilinear. It's made for speed, constant speed that will not exhaust the rider as stop-and-go traffic can and will. Small headlights are not really necessary to ride on well-lit roads . . .

As of now, the chopper is designed with simplicity well-tempered by a certain love for the gaudy.

A classic machine starts out as a "knuckle-head," "shovel-head," or "pan-head" Harley, the most powerful motorcycles put out by the Milwaukee company. In their natural states, they're ugly beasts at best, cantankerous, slow, and full of fat bulges that seem to come from the worst Detroit has to offer. With a top speed of less than a hundred miles an hour, they have no appeal worth mentioning, and even less engineering knowhow.

Like those of most custom vehicles, the chopper engine becomes the center of attraction: a chopper, in fact, cannot be called a chopper unless massive and lavish engine modifications have been made. Since the engines themselves are sometimes already a quarter of a century old or more and have probably weathered a few thousand miles, the modifications are not all for show.

The engines originally displace 1,200 c.c., or roughly the same displacement as a good European sports car. The size can be shot up all the way to 2,000 c.c. by conspicuous reboring and restroking of the cylinders, occasionally leaving them dangerously thin (the result of this can be foreseen: there have been some spectacular engine blowups at red lights, spraying shrapnel left and right and on occasion crippling the would-be drag racer), but since speed is of the essence, danger is overlooked.

Porting and polishing come next, followed by lightening, painting, and finally chroming. Numerous parts will be replaced for more modern and more powerful accessories: camshafts, valves and springs, push rods and pistons, all are sometimes junked, and custom-made or later models' parts are used. Since many Harley parts are interchangeable from year to year, it's a costly but simple chore.

When the engine work is finished, the frame will get the full treatment: it's chopped (hence the name "chopper") and raked to create a much longer wheelbase.

Sharp edges and unnecessary projections are cut off, filed smooth and filled with Fiberglas. The frame can then be molded and generally painted numerous times to achieve a totally smooth appearance.

Since length and thinness favor the searched-for spearlike look, the short, chunky Harley front end is discarded. In its place is bolted a set of springer girders or rigid forks, sometimes up to two feet longer than stock, though the trend is now to shorter front ends. The front brake is removed, though California laws passed in 1971 now require front brakes on all motorcycles

This is a Harley-Davidson "knucklehead" engine, perhaps the most prized engine available to chopper builders. "Knuckleheads" were built by the Milwaukee company from 1937 to 1947.

The details of this Harley chopper were carefully attended to. The paint job was done with some careful airbrush work and overlaid with spatters in contrasting colors. The painted oil tank on this Harley is an unusual detail, as most Harley owners prefer chrome.

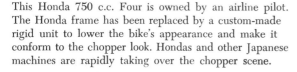

This Honda 750 c.c. Four is owned by an airline pilot. The Honda frame has been replaced by a custom-made rigid unit to lower the bike's appearance and make it conform to the chopper look. Hondas and other Japanese machines are rapidly taking over the chopper scene.

Paint jobs can be simple, as this machine shows. The owner of the knucklehead chose simplicity—a basic color strengthened by a few pinstripes. It's cheaper and sometimes far more effective than costly and outrageous paint jobs.

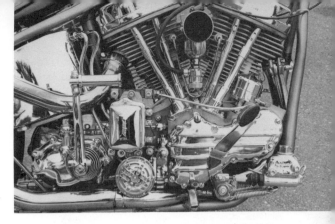

The detailing of this Harley "panhead" (1948 through 1965 models) is spotless, and costly: the owner of this machine has spent a small fortune in chroming alone. The engine is clean, features no loose wiring or oil leaks.

Another "classic" chop. This machine was built primarily for road and not show use. It's simple, yet eye-catching. There are no frills, and the use of chrome is tastefully limited. This machine features a set of "fishtail" exhausts and a "poor boy" sissy bar.

A really well constructed chopper will exhibit careful detailing and some thoughts concerning safety. This is a "classic" machine, a 1200 c.c. Harley-Davidson in a rigid frame. The bike has been kept clean and uncluttered, opting for cleaned up HD lower legs and keeping the front brake for additional stopping power.

The chopper pictured here was also designed with comfort in mind. The tall seat acts as a back rest for passengers and the front brake keeps it safe. The large sixteen-inch rear wheel is standard fare for all choppers.

manufactured after 1960. The removal of the brake serves two purposes: it accentuates the simplicity of the machine and cleans up the look of the front end by getting rid of the unsightly brake cable and hub.

On show-winning machines, the electrical wires are dissimulated through the frame, a complicated job that almost guarantees future problems when short circuits occur.

The seat, sole provider of a Spartan concept of comfort, is padded, but not enough to besmirch the virility of the rider. The seat might be double, to accommodate a passenger who'll be able to avoid unsightly pratfalls by reclining against the sissy bar designed for this purpose.

Most adjuncts of safety are sacrificed for leanness and looks. Volkswagen back-up lights can serve as headlights, and dentists' mirrors, one inch across, will satisfy the letter of the law that states that all motorcycles be equipped with rear-view mirrors.

The rider's originality will be represented by the gas tank, which can be sculptured, chromed, plated, or molded and painted.

Chances are, if you're a discerning buyer with enough loot to afford the best, you'll end up dealing with an amiable young Los Angeles businessman by the name of Tom McMullen.

Tom runs an outfit called AEE choppers, and is famous for riding through the streets of Los Angeles with his wife on an AEE-built machine. It's good advertising, and the chrome-plated shotgun he's said to carry strapped to his back adds a rather interesting touch.

AEE will supply you with every part needed to build your bike from the ground up, and they'll give you a vast choice of different models. Like Detroit automakers, AEE charges according to accessories, and a basic machine composed entirely of their chrome-plated parts can cost a few thousand. No easy credit plan, no monthly payments but preferably cash or at least 50 percent down on a COD order.

They'll give you a vast variety of outlandish seats, frames, front forks, foot pegs. Sissy bars, which for reasons unknown are waning in popularity, are also available. All chrome. Minimum: $45. Since the crowning touch of any chopper is often the exhaust system, AEE is not to be found lacking. There's a wide array of pipes ranging from shorties to six-foot-tall stacks, which properly belong in cathedral organs. But long tails are out this year, too. It seems they do funny things to valves.

AEE is by no means the only company, though it's probably the best-known. Chopper shops that make their own parts and sell them mail-order abound, and a truly dedicated chopper builder will buy a hundred dollars' worth of catalogs before he even starts dismantling his machine. The completed chopper, most likely assembled from a variety of parts made by different companies, will be an eye stopper, but what it has in appeal, it might lack in roadworthiness.

And yet . . . and yet there's probably no rider alive who at one time hasn't wanted to plow his lifesavings into one of these machines, who hasn't wanted to spit in the eye of every motorist on the road by blinding him with mirage-like visions of unleashed and unmanageable horsepower.

There's something about a chopper that defies common sense. Choppers are addictive, like any opiate, and sometimes as dangerous as the worst of the lot. The gut feeling of exhilaration that they provide is largely indescribable to the straighter riders who have mastered the tamer variety of industry built motorcycles.

Their sheer outlandishness, as well as their apparent disregard for the elementary concepts of safety, serves only to enhance their popularity for chopper riders, whether blue-collar gang members or white-collar customizers, are all the same breed, all after the same kick—self-assertion in the face of a too comfortable world. Choppers are machines with built-in defiance, inherent challenge. They are by nature animalistic, pitting your *machismo* against their brute horsepower, your frail musculature against their nonexistent suspension.

Their cost, to an owner, is a major aspect. A chopper is not merely a motorcycle. It's an entity with a personality all its own, a temperament and character that only its owner can fully know, and one demanding constant monetary attention.

Sonny Barger, president of the Hell's Angels motorcycle club in California, once defined love as "what a guy can feel for his bike. . . . Yeah, that's it."

Consider the great majority of chopper owners, often blue-collar workers who are perfectly willing to promptly invest one-third or more of their sweat-earned money back into their machines.

They follow every trend, every new hint of fashion, and will change front ends, paint jobs, and gas tanks several times on each bike to keep up with the times. Chopper spares don't come cheap. Changing a rear wheel

This 1953 Harley panhead was built in too much of a hurry. Sissy bar is unsafe, as are all the loose wires in the engine. Not enough care was taken in rebuilding the engine, and the bike leaks oil badly. Tall seat and "ape hanger" bars are reminiscent of the old chopping days.

can cost more than $250. A minor spill can ruin a chop, bending and twisting sculptured steel worth its weight in gold, scratching paint jobs that can't be touched up. New accessories must be tried, and experiments with $100 engine components are not all that unusual.

The chopper will be treated better than most members of the family. Granddaddy's starving in the bedroom, but the chop needs a new front wheel, and Joe, who hasn't taken a shower in three weeks, has spent his weekend in the garage polishing the beast, lovingly, carefully, inspecting every nook and cranny, getting ready for the week's run.

A great many people have their chopper and nothing else. They support it as others support a family, working just enough to afford a top-end job, a gallon of gas, an oil change.

They'll barter their knowledge for parts, become self-employed for a few short weeks, often in nonspecialized jobs, and earn the money needed for a new paint job more in keeping with the moment's fashion.

The chopper, like most youthful automotive trends, was soon to be fair prey to a horde of largely senseless legislators who saw in the banning of the machine a quick stab at fame and voter appreciation.

Since motorcyclists as a whole have been discriminated against like most minorities, chopper riders, a minority's minority, could not long hope to escape the wrath and logic of state and local lawmakers. The riders are usually members of the lower to middle class, unlearned in the wise politician's ways and therefore incapable of defending themselves against the tide of safety measures being passed by state senates and houses. There never has been, and probably never will be, a chopper lobby in state capitols. Lobbies cost money, money better spent by a club on spare parts or Fourth of July runs.

The Pagans M.C. once did try to lobby against such measures in the nation's capital, no less, and probably caused more harm than good. Club members frightened quite a number of secretaries while trying to find the right office and, upon finding the right office, did not really serve the ranks of motorcyclists. Their club colors, patches, and tattoos, added to the ribald way in which they express themselves, did not impress the legislators favorably. The latter posthaste passed several laws in one sitting, an action not repeated since then. The Pagans roared off into the sunset, sadder but much, much wiser in the ways of the land.

Chopper riders, as a rule, are not voters, and even if they were, their alienation would not particularly harm a potential candidate who based his platform on law and order. The chop people are highly unpopular even among their straighter cycling brethren and downright terrifying to the local citizenry. Their machines make noise, are uncommon, and break speed limits. Most people would place a chopper-straddling, color-packing, foul-smelling, unshaven, and hairy rider somewhere to the right of Attila the Hun.

In Washington, D.C., far removed from the cycling centers of the West Coast, council members quickly passed laws against extended front ends and raked or chopped frames. Maryland vetoed the small and highly popular "buddy seats," terming them unsafe and forbade the use of "nonmanufactured" tailpipes and mufflers.

Both laws were easily side-stepped, since no one really knows what a nonmanufactured tailpipe is, but the ordinances became harassment licenses for any and all law-enforcement officers. Horror stories abound. Riders stopped and hassled for hours on end, forced to dismantle their machines so officers can check serial numbers, forced to tear off Fiberglas molding so that overzealous cops might record frame identifications.

Chopper riders have learned not to take their fights to court. They'll invariably lose, despite expert opinions and witnesses. They cannot be judged by a "jury of their peers" since jury members are registered voters and a large percentage of bikers are not. Their appearance alone is enough to condemn them, and does just that.

Some riders have fooled judges and policemen by cutting their hair, shaving and changing from jeans to suit just before the trial, but as a rule, this is exception rather than practice. A rider's hair is worth more than a $25 fine.

The news factories, both visual and written, have perpetuated the fear of choppers and motorcycles in general by liberally subjecting readers to violent and, more often than not, fictional prose.

A United Press International news dispatch quoted a sheriff as saying, "I have never had any trouble with the local motorcyle gang . . ." The question to ask, then, is why the local group is called a gang. Why not a club, or an organization? When the Shriners don their fezzes and tie up traffic for a couple of hours demonstrating tricky turns on their two-ton Harley dressers, they're called good citizens putting on a show. . . .

Such questions are rarely asked. Typecasting is simple, painless, and satisfying to the millions of readers who daily turn to the obituary pages first. Motorcycle gangs make for good, flashy headlines, better, even, than motorcycle accidents.

The AMA has smugly denied any claim to the choppers, and the overwhelming majority of motorcycle manufacturers have disowned them totally, but enough small companies have made good money peddling Maltese crosses, swastikas, and German World War II helmets, and enough people have discovered that pushing the rough image is profitable, despite what the neighbors think.

The chopper magazines more often than not frown upon the straight rider, deride him in their editorials, and take great pains to destroy the Nicest People image Honda has spent millions of dollars building. Their allegiance belongs not to the AMA, nor to theMotorcycle Industry Council, but to the

This 1972 Yamaha 650 c.c. is a good example of very mild chopping. No modifications were made to the frame, which remains sprung. The machine features a Harley Sportster gas tank, a diamond tuck seat, and a ten-inch front-end extension. The only work done on the engine was the addition of "shorty mufflers."

small group of chop owners and riders who consider themselves the elite of the class.

There are currently a number of strictly chopper-oriented publications, the three leading ones being *Chopper Magazine, Big Bike,* and *Easy Riders.* Both *Big Bike* and *Chopper* are owned by Hi Torque Publishing Company of California; both are unashamedly unreadable to straight riders.

They are inveterate abusers of the clique's jargon and considered the Bible of the chopper set. Sales of both magazines have quadrupled in less than three years and in some places *Chopper* and *Big Bike* have totally outsold the staider *Cycle, Cycle Guide,* and *Cycle World,* going so far as to destroy these magazines' quasi-monopoly and replace them on the newsstands.

The chopper magazines, approximately half grammatical error and half advertising, are written by, for, and about owners. They do not seek to appeal to any other type of rider, to whom their prose is largely undecipherable anyway:

Hill found his '47 Knuck in the back room of a country filling station . . . The stock Harley springers were extended 13 inches and carries 3.00 x 21 Avon on one end and a set of Z bars on 4 inch risers on the other end. The mill lays the power onto the road through a . . .

Their editorials deride the police, the AMA, and the nonchopper rider alike. They're "all Harley" magazines, occasionally breaking down to show a well-chopped Honda Four or Triumph, but such machines are frowned upon and rarely treated with the respect accorded Milwaukee Irons.

The great majority of Japanese bikes are either never mentioned or referred to as "ring-a-dings." Italian machines are called "unforgettable trash."

Nirvana is having a full-color layout of you and your scoot, nestled somewhere in the pages of an upcoming edition, preferably frowning and with appropriate quotes.

Easy Riders is unashamedly for the outlaw rider. It's a far slicker, sex-oriented magazine, with generally better photography and articles than its two rivals, due largely to the fact that until recently it published only once every two months. It has a genuine sense of humor, typified by motorcycle-themed *Playboy*-like cartoons and short stories, pseudo Burt Reynolds fold outs and instructions on how to grow marijuana and make your own "Poorboy Wine," both needed knowledge for the Complete Outlaw.

All three magazines are avidly antilegislation, and all three have done a great deal to further the chopper cause. *Big Bike* recently held a motorcycle show in a state prison, and *Easy Riders* carries a special column dedicated to riders or would-be riders in the clink, along with a modernistic "Dear Abby" column for bikers with sentimental woes.

The California chopper made its bid for social acceptance when Peter Fonda and Dennis Hopper looked for America and, unable to find it, were summarily executed by Southern backwater rednecks. Strangely enough, the machines ridden by the two actors are not good examples of chopper artwork.

Captain America's star-spangled Harley is grossly asymetrical and guilty of major infractions of basic chopper lore. Billy's machine was a standard Harley with an almost stock front end and a stylized flame paint job stolen from someone's little Deuce coupe. Neither machine, if shown now, would elicit the least interest from knowledgeable builders.

But the bikes were enough to persuade untold numbers of riders to adopt the Stars and Stripes motif and go tooling across the land looking for freedom, and the movie in itself was more than enough to create a brand-new industry.

Since then, the bikers' imaginations have ranged from the sublime to the ridiculous. Sonny and Cher own an immaculate Harley Sportster, which illustrates the basic and essential simplicity of all great custom machines. The master of the ridiculous, Ed Roth, long-known for his various contributions to the automotive custom scene, is the designer-owner of a one thousand-pound, 289 cubic inch Ford V-8 chopper trike, parts of which he will sell to anyone interested.

Jim Lytle, a California rodder, purchased an Air Force Surplus twenty-two-cylinder Allison airplane engine, and for lack of a place to put it, stuffed it between Harley, Ford, and Mercury parts to create the world's most famous fearsome tricycle. To date, no one has ever ridden it.

In February, 1971, *Esquire* magazine heralded the chopper as the decade's contribution to kinetic art. Tom Wolfe went a wee bit overboard in depicting some of Tom McMullen's and Howard McCall's machines:

The original outlook (of the chopper builders) was kinetic, and their artistic sense followed from that. Quite independently of Duchamp, the chopper builders realized the design possibilities of the wheel and took it a step beyond Duchamp's insight . . .

Joe Namath sat grinningly atop one of McMullen's bikes looking exactly like a football player sitting on a chopper.

Quite a few people laughed and at least one wrote an unpublished and unflattering letter to the editor. The rest asked what kinetic art was, anyway.

The chopper had come the full circle, from outlaw machine to pop art. It was inevitable that, once treated as art, it be degraded by the dubious honor of having a television show based around it. A series named *Then Came Bronson* appeared, depicting an itinerant young man of unknown age and trade who crisscrossed the West upon a red Harley Sportster. The gist of the serial was that the Harley seemed to have magical powers: it was undoubtedly the only Harley-Davidson motorcycle ever made that could mysteriously change engines when needed. As such, it featured a V-twin when jamming along the highways, and a single when scrambling. It always won, and Harley dealers reported having a very hard time keeping the 900 c.c. Sportster in stock. Models customized to approximate the Bronson chop sold out immediately.

In the past few years, since the exporting of Honda's powerful four-cylinder 750 c.c. motorcycle, choppers have been diverging. The Honda 750 has become the favorite of an entire school of builders who have found in the well-engineered Japanese import a respite from the Harley faults. Most chopper accessory companies now sell a wide range of parts for Hondas, Yamahas, Triumphs, and BSAs, and the word chopper no longer means strictly Harley-Davidson. Virtually every machine with a raised front end or a sissy bar is now called a chop, thereby bastardizing the concept while opening up new vistas of creation. AEE sells parts that will make a Honda 450 c.c. into a chopper, and the old school of cycle customizing has taken some strong knocks. Even the hard-core chopper magazines have reluctantly admitted that Japanese and British machines do have their strong points, though some riders have expressed concern over the future of the trend.

The true Harley chopper, of course, will die. Its death is as inevitable as that of the hot rod and will come in much the same way: industry will not allow a profitable venture to be overlooked and the days of the garage customizer are already at an end.

More powerful machines are coming out, machines that with half the engine size will wipe out the chop at the lights, better designed motorcycles that will cost half as much and go twice as fast.

Norton-Villiers, in the first half of 1971, put out an absurd parody of the chopper called the High Rider. It was a stock Norton Commando to which had been bolted high-rise handlebars, a sissy bar, and a ridiculous camel seat, which would not please even an American posterior.

Harley-Davidson betrayed its own by selling its most faithful adherents down the river with the production of a large displacement monstrosity nicknamed the "Night Train." Basically a skinny version of the ever popular Electra Glide, the Train features a slimmed-down front end and a paint job highly nostalgic of 1950 hot-rod days. As a motorcycle, the Night Train is some twenty years behind the rest of the industry's technology, and even among Harley freaks thought to be a loser. Its design is prehistoric, its handling and braking atrocious. As a chopper, though, the machine will probably sell, for the basic traits of the custom motorcycle are there and the resemblance to the real thing is enough to fool the unwary.

The chop of the future? Perhaps. Many custom builders are now turning their attention to "trikes." The trike is half-motorcycle, half-car, all imagination. Trikes generally start out as Harley-Davidson three wheelers, but many companies are presently manufacturing attachments which enable a bike owner to make a trike from his machine. A trike is more stable, more comfortable, and often more powerful than a standard chopper.

And the Harley chopper will die, too, when its price outweighs its worth: as old Harleys become rarities and increase in value, so will builders sway from the custom machine and come to rely on manufactured replicas, and as changes and style trends come too quickly and expensively, so will riders decide that perhaps, after all, the "true" chopper has had its day.

8

Freud Never Had
a Motorcycle Anyway . . .

"Four wheels good, two wheels bad." The concept first mentioned in George Orwell's *Animal Farm* in 1945 hasn't vanished, though the past four or five years have seen it diminish somewhat in strength and righteousness. The advent of the small motorcycle has palled the reputation of the bigger machines, yet it's a rare individual who, upon first contact with a motorcycle, will not spout off some second- or third-hand opinion girdled in phallic Freudianisms. Bikers have been accused of virtually every psychological sin and hang up so far manufactured by man, and the sport and pleasure of cycling have both undoubtedly suffered from the numerous theories advanced regarding the psychological make-up of riders.

In fact, little if anything has been proven, and though many are willing to swear that So-and-So's Yamaha is nothing more than an extension of his manhood, few have been able to match theory and fact.

Again, *The Wild One* can probably be held responsible for the furtherance if not the birth of the various myths attributed both to riders and machines. Whether Johnny was sexually inadequate we'll never know, but we can assume that he was a troubled lad whose motorcycle represented

149

far more than any steel and iron piece of machinery should. *On Any Sunday* largely tended to avoid the Wild One image and focused instead on the all-American aspect of motorcycling as a family sport and pastime, and *Easy Rider* saw the chopped Harleys as a means of attaining freedom. All three interpretations are right, yet all three fall far short of the mark that encompasses the total concept of biking.

Motorcycles are all the above, but then so is virtually every means of self-expression, every sport, every hobby. A gathering of radio-controlled-airplane buffs will not ire the populace, and it's a sure bet that the checkers federation could hold its annual tournaments virtually anywhere in the world without getting the local militia hot and bothered. Baseball teams have never been thrown out of town, philatelists have never been hassled by the forces of law and order. Yet motorcyclists draw criticisms as honey draws flies. In seeking to explode misconceptions, one must first find their basis for existence. And in finding the basis, one must delve into the psychology not only of the myth's subjects but also the myth's creator. The average nonbiking citizen does have an opinion about the machines that roar or whine past him. There might be envy tinged with annoyance at the noise that can and often does shatter peace. There might simply be lack of comprehension. There's often antagonism.

Why? Bikes, per se, are simply modes of transportation, a refinement of the bicycle, a step short of an automobile. They're not as noisy as large trucks or jets, not as cumbersome as buses. But they are . . . different. As are their riders.

The established have always viewed the different with a wary eye, often refusing to really analyze but reacting with a gut emotion untouched by rationality. What is different is threatening, a step away from the customary and the usual, a dim awareness that perhaps what is accepted is not really what is best. But acceptance is hard to come by, and individuality is a paradoxical thing: everyone looks for it, but few people accept it in others, particularly if the individuality is manifested in a fashion too far removed from the accepted. A wide tie is original, amusing and individual when everyone's wearing shoestring ties and few people will actively criticize the person who wears one. The action is not threatening, and the smile will be condescending but not hostile. As the unusual drifts from the accepted to the unaccepted, hostilities tend to rise with almost mathematical precision. Hostilities decrease when the unaccepted becomes accepted, as it most often does, until the process is repeated once again.

Motorcycles are now on the upswing, and as such are regarded as objects that have not quite yet established their social cubbyhole. Small, brightly colored machines making little noise and ridden by sanitary people are accepted. Bigger machines, particularly customized machines, are not. The problem of acceptance is complicated by the fact that big-bike riders are often weird birds, steeped in their own aura and wildly devoted to their machines, a devotion that is largely misunderstood, misinterpreted, and vulnerable to virtually any and all theory. A thorough check of the Library of Congress, the American Medical Association, the American Psychological Association, the American Psychiatric Association, and numerous other organizations that should have yielded a wealth of information concerning the average biker's psyche yielded nothing. In short, few if any knowledgeable treatises on the psychology of motorcycling have as yet been advanced, which presents an interesting question: where do all the theories come from? Possibly the bikers themselves. Many a rider has, at one time or another, felt what can only be described as a devotion for his machine.

Freewheeling Frank, secretary of the Hell's Angels, recounted in a book named after him the anger and frustration he felt at seeing his motorcycle "manhandled" by policemen as he lay on the ground almost unconscious. Yet few riders look upon their machines as quasi-human entities with the fanaticism manifested by outlaw club members. Indeed, the greater percentage of bikers regard motorcycles as what they are, vehicles that are fun, individualistic to an extent, and ever so slightly addictive. No biker can deny the rush of emotions engendered by riding.

A rider's attachment to his cycle might in fact be nothing more than a driver's feelings for his automobile earlier in the century when cars were not as common as they are today, taken much less matter of factly than they are now. Owners of certain sports cars have the same attachments, particularly the outrageously expensive imports owned by a lucky few. Added to the basic desire to keep a possession in good working order is one often overlooked fact: a bike needs one hell of a lot more upkeep than most cars do. The engine, the electrics, the entire steering assembly, seat, gas tanks, and wheels are totally exposed to the elements, to the whims of temperature and humidity. Constant and unrelenting care is needed if the beast is to start every morning. And a dirty motorcycle looks plain ratty and will have a tendency to rub off some of its dirt on the rider. Few are the bikers who at one time or another have not experienced a disastrous oil or gas leak, one that totally destroyed pants, shirts, and underwear.

One of the rare studies that might give a certain insight into the biker personality was conducted by Dr. Patricia F. Waller of the University of North Carolina Highway Safety Research Center. Titled "Motorcycles Versus Automobiles: How Do Their Owners Differ," the report comparing motorcycle to automobile-owning students, effectively destroys the black-leather image and goes on to state:

. . . we found that motorcycle students were less likely to be in graduate or professional school, less likely to be married, and more likely to be out of state than were the automobile students. In terms of grades, we found no difference between motorcycle and automobile students . . . the motorcycle students on the whole looked just as healthy as the automobile students with the possible exception of a higher score on the paranoid scale . . . for the motorcycle student (but) it may well be that this one finding can be attributed to chance factors *and does not reflect a real difference between the two groups* . . . [italics mine].

Both bikers and car drivers, in other words, reflected basically the same results. One particularly interesting discovery reported by Dr. Waller is that both motorcycle and automobile students seemed to manifest healthier and more stable personalities than did the student population in general. "A possible explanation for this finding is in terms of socioeconomic status, that is, students with wheels tend to be somewhat better off financially, and higher socioeconomic status is related to healthier personality test records." No phallic symbols, sexual gratification, overt or covert homosexuality were mentioned in the report.

Public attitude must change. It will have to, as the number of bikers increase and the cyclist comes to be considered no stranger than the car driver. It will also change when car drivers, who represent the greatest danger to both the motorcycle's safety and reputation, are trained to recognize bikes as equals. And finally, it will change when people realize that chrome, metal, padded upholstery, and power steering are not prerequisite to normalcy.

Ride on.

Freedom . . . perhaps that's what biking is all about, the chance to soar over hills, up in the air, and down hard. This rider, incidentally, is in for a shock when he lands. Sitting during a jump is one of the better ways of acquiring multiple pains. Riding in the boondocks in a short-sleeved shirt isn't recommended either.

Index

74 75 76 77 10 9 8 7 6 5 4 3 2 1